SUPERBOY & SUPERPUP

THE LOST VIDEOS

by CHUCK HARTER

Copyright © 1993 by Chuck Harter

All rights reserved. No part of this book may be reproduced or transmitted in any form or by any means, electronic or mechanical, including photocopying, recording or by any informational storage or retrieval system -- except by a reviewer who may quote brief passages in a review to be printed in a magazine or newspaper -- without permission in writing from the publisher. For information and/or inquiries, contact:

BearManor Media • 4700 Millenia Blvd. • Suite 175 PMB 90497 • Orlando, Florida 32839

Although the author and publisher have exhaustively researched all sources to ensure the accuracy and completeness of the information contained in this book, we assume no responsibility for errors, inaccuracies, omissions or any inconsistency herein. Any slights of people or organizations are unintentional. Readers should consult an attorney or accountant for specific application to their individual publishing ventures.

Superman characters and Superman name are registered trademarks of D.C. Comics Inc. All visuals are used for illustrative purposes only and no infringement on the rights of copyright holders intended.

Library of Congress Cataloging in Publication Data

Harter, Chuck
    Superboy & Superpup -- The Lost Videos

Copyright Registration Number: TXu 509 427

This edition published in the USA by:
BearManor Media • 4700 Millenia Blvd. • Suite 175 PMB 90497 • Orlando, Florida 32839
www.bearmanormedia.com

Hardcover: ISBN 978-1-62933-905-4
Paperback: ISBN 978-1-62933-904-7

ACKNOWLEDGEMENTS

The author would like to express much gratitude to the following for their interviews and help:

    Joe Biroc -- cinematographer on "Superpup"

    Ben Chapman -- production manager on "Superpup" and "Superboy"

    Virginia Clark -- daughter of "Superboy" co-author Vernon Clark

    Frank Delfino -- Sergeant Beagle in *The Adventures Of Superpup*

    Ruth (Delfino) Spering -- Pamela Poodle in *The Adventures Of Superpup*

    Sadie Delfino -- Wolfingham in *The Adventures Of Superpup*

    Jane Ellsworth -- wife (widow) of producer Whit Ellsworth

    Patricia (Ellsworth) Wilson -- daughter of producer Whit Ellsworth

    Cal Howard -- director of "Superpup"

    Ronnie James -- television historian

    Dick Rawlings -- cinematographer on "Superboy"

    John Rockwell -- Superboy in *The Adventures Of Superboy*

    Mel Shaw -- designer and maker of "Superpup" masks

    Si Simonson -- special effects technician on "Superpup" and "Superboy"

    Art Weissman -- George (Superman) Reeves' personal manager

Many thanks also, to the following for their assistance: Forry Ackerman, Bill Armstrong, Gary Barbuto, Michael Bifulco, Dave Brewton, Dan Capitoli, Gary Coddington, Miles Davis, Omega Demissie, Linda J. Ehrlich, Richard Ervais, Dean Finch, Randy Garrett, Bruce Hamilton, Charles W. Harter, Luella Harter, Rob Harvey, Jan Alan Henderson, Hollywood Book & Poster Co., Ken Holmes, Leo Jiminez, Henry Lozano, Vince Marzo, Gwen Meades, Jerry Neeley, Paragon Photos, Charlie Parker, Don Peterson, Quantity Photos, Inc., George Reeves, Jane Regner, Viv Savage, Howard Teman, Natividad Vacio, and Leni Wander.

And a *special* thanks to those super-men, John Field, Jim Hambrick, Michael J. Hayde and Jim Nolt for their invaluable assistance -- you guys are "real George."

And super-special thanks to Mike Copner and Buddy Barnett for their faith and vision.

BOOK AND COVER DESIGNED BY CHUCK HARTER

All photographs and illustrations in this book, except as noted, are from the collection of Chuck Harter.

Artwork: Dean Finch, back cover; Randy Garrett, pp. 100, 106, 116, 118; Ken Holmes, pp. 110, 112, 120, 122; Leo Jiminez (artwork)/Ken Holmes (inking), pp. 102, 104, 108, 114
Typography: Fantastically FYIRS

FOREWORD

by Michael J. Hayde

What are *The Adventures Of Superpup* (1958) and *The Adventures Of Superboy* (1961), besides the obvious answer of two unaired television pilots? And why a book to chronicle their history?

The answer to both questions is the same. Both pilots are important parts of the "Superman" legend, especially as it pertains to the classic, long running television series starring George Reeves. And yet, despite the burgeoning interest in science fiction and comic book heroes, slight attention has been given to these "super" spin-offs. What little exists has been both perfunctory and opinionated.

This is probably due to a naive belief that nobody would be interested. Indeed, when Chuck Harter told me that he was planning to write this book, I was skeptical to say the least. Even as a diehard fan of *The Adventures Of Superman,* I couldn't see how an entire book about these two pilots could hold much interest to me. What was there to say?

A lot. I soon learned, through Chuck's scholarly efforts, that both pilots deserve much more than an opinionated passing nod. They stand as admirable attempts to expand on the success of the Reeves television show. "Superpup," filmed on the same sets as "Superman," attempts to appeal to a *Captain Kangaroo* audience too young to appreciate the Man Of Steel. (More than one observer may notice a similarity between "Superpup" and an animated cartoon hero of the sixties named "Underdog.") As for "Superboy," this was a full scale attempt to capture the "Superman" audience with new adventures of their hero as a boy. "Superboy" looked so promising that 13 shooting scripts were completed. Yet, nearly 30 years would pass before "Superboy" was given the chance to fly on television.

In seeking out the full story behind these "lost videos," Chuck conducted several interviews with surviving cast and crew members, researched production information, located the shooting scripts (including the 12 "Superboy" scripts that were never filmed), and -- most importantly -- unearthed dozens of never-before-seen photographs taken on the sets of both shows. These photos help to reveal the behind-the-scenes action, including preparation for special effects shots. All of this material is presented in a highly informative and highly entertaining book, which should appeal to anyone interested in "Superman," or comic book heroes, or television production...in short, a wide audience.

Most of all, the book is a tribute to the talents of a man that "Superman" fans know well: producer Whitney Ellsworth. When Mr. Ellsworth, editorial director for National (now D.C.) Comics, assumed the producer's chair for "Superman" in 1953, he brought to the show his ideals, his love for children, and his sense of humor. Naturally, these qualities were also present in the two pilots (which were, of course, Ellsworth's own creations). Latter day critics have not been very kind in their assessment of the "Ellsworth approach," wishing instead that Whit had kept "Superman" in the one-dimensional mold of violent crime-buster. But, Ellsworth was never one-dimensional, and this book does much to set the record straight.

Technically, the "Superpup" and "Superboy" pilots are no longer "lost." Videocassettes of both have been available in a limited capacity for several years; sold by underground manufacturers who specialize in public domain material. Interest in these pilots, and their role in the history of the "Superman" legend exists, and although the pilots themselves won't be found at the neighborhood video store, they can be seen today, provided one knows where to look. It's the true story of how and why they were made that has never been made available...until now.

At last, a part of the "Superman" legend that has remained under wraps for over 30 years, is now ready to be told: the story of "Superboy" and "Superpup," the lost videos.

MICHAEL J. HAYDE
is a television historian who
resides in the Los Angeles area.

DEDICATION

*To my mother and father, Luella and Chuck Harter;
thank you for your love, faith and hope.*

. . . and . . .

To Gwen Meades, for her hard work and dedication to this book.
...and may she find that cabin someday.

TABLE OF CONTENTS

Chapter 1: MR. WHITNEY ELLSWORTH . . . .

Chapter 2: THE ADVENTURES OF SUPERPUP
(THE STORY) . . . .

Chapter 3: THE MAKING OF SUPERPUP . . . .

Chapter 4: THE ADVENTURES OF SUPERBOY
(THE STORY -- RAJAH'S RANSOM) . . .

Chapter 5: THE PRODUCTION OF SUPERBOY . . . .

Chapter 6: THE SERIES THAT MIGHT HAVE BEEN
(THE TWELVE UNFILMED
SUPERBOY SCRIPTS) . . . .

SUMMARY . . . .

Good Comic Publishers Resent 'Fly-by-Nighters'

Editorial Director of Superman Answers Critics of Kid Books

If your kid is driving you crazy with comic books and you have grave fears for his morals and manners, take heart. Your young will not go to the dogs as the result of reading "Superman" any more than you did after having devoured every "Nick Carter" book that was ever written.

In fact, "comics magazines are a natural outgrowth of newspaper comics, an integral part of the folklore and culture of America," Whitney Ellsworth, editorial director for the largest group of comics magazines, the Superman D. C. group, told The Herald this week.

"The decent ones are here to stay," he added.

"Like the dime thrillers of a generation ago, they are an answer to the constant, generation-after-generation seeking for the hero and his exploits, the vicarious satisfaction of the yearning of the average guy for participation in great and fine deeds of derring-do in which he can actually never be a participant.

OPPORTUNISTS BLAMED

"In short, the same sort of satisfaction he has always gained in every fictional form, be it the novel, the stage, the screen or whatever."

Moved to the defense of his own medium by recent, vitriolic criticism of comics magazines in newspapers, magazines and on the air, Ellsworth, a Greenwich resident, charged that the responsibility for the present feeling about comics in general lies with a comparatively few publishers, Johnny-come-latelies who are more interested in quick profits than in competing honestly for a share of sales in a legitimate market.

Pointing out that it is unfair to place all comics in the same classification, just as it is unfair to condemn all movies, radio shows or books because certain movies, radio shows or books are in questionable taste, Ellsworth explained:

CLEAN ADVENTURE

"The great majority of comics magazines offer clean adventure stories, interestingly and excitingly told in a graphic medium. In our own organization we try especially to inject educational material into the stories themselves. Conversely, we endeavor to keep out anything of an objectionable nature."

To insure a clean and wholesome product. National Comics Publications employs an editorial staff of nine persons who hold writers and artists to a rigid editorial policy.

In addition the editors have the counsel of an editorial advisory board whose members include Josette Frank, consultant on children's reading, Child Study Assn. of America; Dr. Lauretta Bender, associate professor of psychiatry, New York university school of medicine; Dr. C. Bowie Millican, member of New York university's department of English literature; Dr. W. W. D. Sones, professor of education and director of curriculum study, University of Pittsburgh and Dr. S. Harcourt Peppard, acting director, bureau of child guidance, New York city board of education.

GOOD AND BAD

Psychologists and educators who complain about the effects of comics on children "haven't learned to differentiate between the good and the bad," Ellsworth said.

"We hear a good deal of talk about psycho-this and psycho-that in connection with comics, but I don't think normally-adjusted children are going to be hurt any more by decent comics than we were in our generation by the dime novels."

In the end, the comics question is up to the parents, Ellsworth points out.

"A youngster can have too much ice cream, too much radio, too much movie-going, and, admittedly, too much comics-reading," says the 39-year-old editor.

"I feel it's part of a parent's duty to instill in the child not only a sense of discrimination between the acceptable and the unacceptable, but also a sense of proportion."

How can a parent distinguish between good and bad comics?

"The line of demarcation between highly objectionable and somewhat objectionable comics on the one hand, and acceptable comics on the other, narrows down to a simple fundamental, good taste," explained Ellsworth.

The differences between good and bad comics magazines are explained by Whitney Ellsworth of Greenwich, editorial director of the country's largest group of magazines, the Superman D. C. outfit.

Whit Ellsworth in his office at the corporate headquarters of D.C. Comics, New York City, 1944

Newspaper article by Whit Ellsworth, 1948 (pre-Comics Code)

Chapter 1

MR. WHITNEY ELLSWORTH

(PRODUCER OF SUPERBOY & SUPERPUP)

Frederick Whitney Ellsworth was born in Brooklyn, New York on November 27, 1908. He was educated at the Polytechnic Preparatory Country Day School in Brooklyn and graduated in 1926. Soon after, he took a cartooning course at the Brooklyn Y.M.C.A. under Ad Carter, later his assistant. His first professional work, in the late 1920's was as a gag writer and assistant on such King Features newspaper strips as *Tillie The Toiler, Dumb Dora* and *Embarrassing Moments*. In the early 1930's, Whit worked for two New Jersey newspapers, the Newark Star-Eagle and the Newark Ledger in various capacities including cartooning, reporting and feature writing. While working for several pulp magazines, he wrote a play entitled *Maiden Voyage* in 1935 which was produced in New York and enjoyed a short Off-Broadway run.

1935 was also the year that Malcolm Wheeler-Nicholson, a pulp magazine publisher, fused the stories used in his pulps with the adventures comic strips that were beginning to be seen in newspapers. These efforts, the first prototype of the comic books, were in black and white and were tabloid sized.

Whit's daughter, Patricia Ellsworth Wilson, recently recalled his first involvement with the comic book field which would play such a large part in his life:

> "My father was one of the triumvirate of editors who worked for Major Nicholson on the very first original comics magazines that were. That was in the middle 1930's...and the triumvirate consisted of Whitney Ellsworth, Craig Flessel and Vincent Sullivan. The owner of the group was Major Nicholson. Somewhere, maybe '37 or '38, D.C. Comics (Detective Comics) bought out Nicholson and in 1937 Whitney Ellsworth left New York completely and went to live in Hollywood for a couple of years."

On September 24, 1938, Whit married Jane Dewey, who was under contract to Paramount and had appeared in such features as *Wells Fargo, Ruler of the Seas* and *If I Were King*. In 1940, D.C. Comics head Jack Liebowitz hired Whit as the editorial director. Whit returned to New York and began working for the fledgling firm.

Patricia Ellsworth Wilson:

> "It was a pretty rudimentary operation when he was asked to join it. What he did from that point was to hire the whole editorial department. The reason that he was skilled in knowing which people to hire was that he had been a cartoonist, pulp writer and comics writer. He created many of D.C.'s characters, but he never in fact created any of the leading ones. He was involved in 80 percent of the development of the stories that went into the magazines."

Around this time Whit drew several of D.C.'s covers such as *New Comics* and was allowed to sign his name, an honor at the time.

Jane Ellsworth, Whit's wife, recently commented on his early days at D.C. Comics:

> "He hired the people who became the editors such as Mort Weisinger (story editor on *The Adventures Of Superboy* pilot), Jack Schiff, Murray Belsinor and others. Whit did practically everything and was actually quite popular with the writers and artists. He always went to bat for them, getting them more money and stuff like that."

In 1941, Whit traveled to Florida to act as an advisor on the critically acclaimed Fleischer Studios Superman cartoons. These 17 full color cartoons, originally released by Paramount Pictures, are hailed today as some of the finest examples of the animator's art. Their fidelity to Siegel and Schuster's conception of the Superman character are almost without parallel, including the many and varied interpretations that have since followed.

Whit began writing the *Superman* daily and Sunday newspaper strips in 1941 due to Jerry Siegel's being drafted into the Army, and continued to do so throughout 1945. During the mid- to late-1940's, Whit would periodically go to California to advise Columbia studios on their serial adaptations of several D.C. Comics' characters. These included *Batman* (1943), *Superman* 1948, *Batman and Robin* (1949), *Congo Bill* (1949) and *Atom Man Vs. Superman* (1950). *Congo Bill*, in fact, was Whit's own creation. These serials' fidelity to the original characters varied, which tends to make one believe that the powers that were at Columbia didn't really listen to Whit's suggestions, unlike the Fleischer

SUPERBOY & SUPERPUP - THE LOST VIDEOS

L-R: Whit Ellsworth, wife Jane Ellsworth, National Comics President Harry Donenfeld, Virginia Bliss, daughter Patricia Ellsworth; at RKO-Pathe Studios, Culver City, California during the filming of "Superman And The Mole Men," 1951

"The Adventures Of Superman" producer Whitney Ellsworth and production manager Clem Beauchamp at the Superman, Inc. Office on the California Studios Lot, 1953

MR. WHITNEY ELLSWORTH

Studios of the early 1940's. However, the serials, especially the two featuring the Superman character and starring Kirk Alyn, were among the most popular and profitable in the history of the genre.

In the late 1940's Whit publicly established an editorial code policy for D.C. Comics which pre-dated the official Comics Code of 1953, and had been in effect since Whit's becoming editorial director in 1940. During the 1940's, comics were considered by many to be second class literature or, in extreme cases, to cause juvenile delinquency. Many parental groups levied a great deal of criticism toward "funny books" as well as the people who worked on them. Whit always defended the books and established D.C.'s own editorial policy as a means of reassuring anxious parents that their children's reading material was not harmful. (See article by Whit at beginning of this chapter.)

Patricia Ellsworth Wilson:

> "He had these rules of behavior in the comics...he was top dog in that company (D.C.) on the creative side. He wouldn't have let anything gory go in anything that he had anything to do with. My father's personality was one of great innocence and humor, and respect for children as human beings."

Jane Ellsworth:

> "He wasn't much more than a kid himself. Cartoonists are a breed apart. For one thing, they never really grow up, and they are funny, and, as Bill Cosby might say, "they think funny." That was part of Whit's personality. His philosophy in regard to the comic books was that they were for children; that they should be fun, clean, non-violent, and that the English should always be correct...he did allow for some slang. This is pretty much what became the so-called "Comics Code of 1953-54," and it stood D.C. Comics in good stead when the national investigation into violence in the comic books occurred."

In 1951, Whit came back to California to advise and co-write the script for Lippert Pictures' *Superman And The Mole Men*, starring George Reeves and Phyllis Coates. He co-wrote the screenplay with producer Robert Maxwell under the pen name of Richard Fielding. This modest feature film's success was due primarily to the conviction of George Reeves' and Phyllis Coates' acting and to the script, which was a plea for equality and understanding among people. The film also served as an introduction to a new actor, Reeves, as Superman, and to the upcoming television series. Concurrently, production of the first season of *The Adventures Of Superman* was being filmed on the RKO-Pathe Studios lot. Whit acted in an advisory capacity to Producer Robert Maxwell during "Superman's" production. These dark, violent episodes were an immediate hit with viewers of early television, and were directed at adults watching during the evening hours. The series was sponsored by Kellogg's Cereals through the Leo Burnett Agency.

In 1953, after Robert Maxwell's departure due to artistic differences, Whit left his position as editorial director of D.C. Comics and became producer of *The Adventures Of Superman*. Maxwell's radio based murder mysteries (he had produced the '40's Superman radio shows) gave way to a format which came more from the comic book stories.

Patricia Ellsworth Wilson:

> "My father's approach was that the character Superman on television should reflect the character in the D.C. comics. That it was a translation to the screen of that character. He always felt that comics magazines were aimed at children and teenagers and so he conceived that the TV show was also aimed at children and teenagers, and he would not have been in favor of very dark, blood-thirsty plots."

Whit, as producer, in pursuing his vision of the Superman legend, fought from the beginning for the best values possible from the limited budget he had to work with.

Around this time, Dr. Fredrick Wertham published his stinging attack on comics entitled *Seduction Of The Innocent*. This caused a major crackdown on the comic book industry which resulted in several companies going out of business and some such as E.C Comics, altering their own editorial policies. D.C. Comics were not subjected to much criticism due to the foresight of Whit's editorial policies of several years before.

These policies were extended to the 1953 season of Superman and were undoubtedly justified due to the continued rise in popularity of the TV show.

The production company, now called Superman, Inc., had moved to California Studios and Whit, along with Production Manager Clem Beauchamp, oversaw filming. The new format saw the show rise to tremendous heights of popularity with children. A large part of this surge in popularity was due to the rapport of cast members Jack Larson (Jimmy Olsen), Noel Neill (Lois Lane), John Hamilton (Perry White), Robert Shayne (Inspector Henderson), and to the warmth and believability of George Reeves in the dual role of Clark Kent and Superman. Although he got along well with all the cast members, Whit had a special relationship with George Reeves that transcended the usual one of producer and star.

Patricia Ellsworth Wilson:

> "My father was very fond of George, and

SUPERBOY & SUPERPUP - THE LOST VIDEOS

"Superman" star George Reeves and Whit Ellsworth celebrate Whit's birthday in his production office at ZIV Studios, November 27, 1956.

Laughs on the ZIV lot. Whit Ellsworth and Superman (George Reeves)
(Bottom two photos courtesy of Jim Hambrick)

Whit and George on the "Superman" set. Whit quote: "Our relationship was always a warm and friendly one."

MR. WHITNEY ELLSWORTH

George in fact, called my father "Dad." They were close friends. Whit admired him. He felt that he was an absolute pro. George was just a great worker. He always knew his lines, he was always in good shape, he always delivered, and my father appreciated that a lot."

Whit himself said in a letter to a Superman TV show fan, Jim Nolt:

"George was friendly and charming. Our relationship was always a warm and friendly one."

In 1954, along with Superman's third season of filming, Whit produced two outside projects. The first was five Superman feature films which were comprised of three episodes each of the 1953 season with some linking scenes, newly shot for continuity. They were designed for the British market and were shown throughout England. As released by 20th Century Fox, titles included *Superman's Peril, Superman Flies Again, Superman In Exile, Superman And Scotland Yard*, and *Superman And The Jungle Devil*. Whit's other project that year was the production of three pilot films for a projected series call *The American*. Based on Whit's strong interest in American history, the films starred William Lundigan as a sort of "every-man" on the fringe of different events in American history. They were made by Lexington Productions, which appears to have been an offshoot of Superman, Inc. Titles included *A Friend In New York* (based on the Boston Tea Party), *Indian Boy* (set in the wilderness) and *Time Of Battle* (a Civil War tale). The reason that three were shot may have been with the intention of splicing them together much like the five Superman features that played in Great Britain. Sadly, although Whit did receive the budget to make the pilots, when it came time to pitch them to the networks, the packager suddenly backed out and the project was stalled. In retrospect, it could have been a unique series.

Patricia Ellsworth Wilson:

"William Lundigan would have played an ongoing character in different periods of history. He would have a different name and be a different person, but he would always be the typical American. This was the ordinary American man and dramatic situations would affect him throughout different periods of history."

In 1954, prior to the third season of Superman's filming, still at California Studios, Whit had the foresight to have the shows shot in color. The final four seasons were filmed in color, but were not broadcast that way at the time. Once again, Whit was forced to work within a limited budget.

From a letter written by Whit Ellsworth to Jim Nolt:

"I had talked our sponsor, Kellogg's, into shooting in color and picking up the extra expense just as a sort of hedge against a possible day when they might wish to telecast them in color, but the cost of making duplicate color negatives, the necessary first step in making color prints, was so high that we went directly to B & W prints."

In fact, none of the Superman shows were shown in color until 1965 when the series enjoyed renewed popularity due to the color telecasts. Whit's vision and foresight had paid off and the episodes are still being shown today in many markets.

The Adventures Of Superman continued in production during the 1955 season (at the Chaplin Studios) and the 1956 season (on the ZIV Studios lot). The series continued to grow in popularity with the 1956 season gaining the highest ratings of the entire run. The sixth and last season of Superman was filmed from September to November 1957. The series had enjoyed a healthy six year stay and had, in fact, gone from syndication to the ABC network for the final season.

During mid-November 1957, one week after Superman finished filming, Whit produced a color pilot entitled *The Adventures Of Superpup* at ZIV Studios. Geared to the 7-year and under age group, the pilot, though well intentioned, was not picked up for broadcast. (For the complete story behind the shooting, see *Chapter 3 - The Making Of Superpup*.)

Whit continued to write scripts for television productions during this time and sold several stories to such shows as *The Millionaire*. Due to the increasing popularity of the Superman reruns, by early 1959, Whit had convinced the home office to option a new season of 26 Superman episodes. In early June, acceptance of the new season had been confirmed by the New York office of National Periodical Publications and on June 15, 1959, Whit telephoned George Reeves to inform him that the series was "on." George was thrilled. Tragically, the next evening, George Reeves was found dead from a gunshot wound to the head and all plans for the new season were canceled.

In 1961, Whit produced a live-action black and white pilot for a proposed syndicated series entitled *The Adventures Of Superboy*, also at ZIV Studios. Although an interesting production, it was also not picked up for broadcast. (For the complete story behind the pilot, see *Chapter 5 - The Production Of Superboy - "Rajah's Ransom."*)

After the finalization of the two super-hero pilots, Whit concentrated on his writing. He wrote several humorous pieces for publication, one of which, *My Mother, The Witch*, appeared in the November 12, 1966 issue of TV Guide. Other articles appeared in daily newspapers and

SUPERBOY & SUPERPUP - THE LOST VIDEOS

"The Adventures of Superboy" star, John Rockwell and producer Whit Ellsworth on location in Bronson Canyon, Griffith Park, California, April 4, 1961

MR. WHITNEY ELLSWORTH

Sunday supplements. He did make one final foray into television and began work as a consultant on the 1966 *Batman* TV series. However, he soon left after disagreeing with the "campy" concept of the show.

Patricia Ellsworth Wilson:

> *"My father was put on that show as a consultant. I don't think he even worked there for a week. Because he and the producers disagreed totally on how to do the show, and he was supposed to be an advisor and nobody would listen. To camp up the show, in his view, insulted the conception and the characters."*

He wrote for the Batman newspaper strip from 1966-1970 and wrote on and off for the Superman newspaper strip until 1970.

In declining health, he retired from National Periodical Publications in 1971 and settled in Westlake Village, California. Though his physical condition had weakened, he continued to write and kept active in a creative way. Whit also continued drawing cartoons, and particularly enjoyed drawing the Ellsworths' yearly Christmas cards which he had done from 1937 until 1979, the year before his passing.

He was gratified with the Superman TV show's continuing popularity in reruns, but was mildly upset at the cutting of them for extra commercial time.

Patricia Ellsworth Wilson:

> *"He was thrilled that it (the show) went on and on. He was delighted. But then when they went into syndication, he was unhappy because they were cut so much. He said that his years as the producer of Superman were the happiest of his professional life, so he'd be happy that they continue."*

In the mid-1970's he wrote for and advised Noel Neill (Lois Lane) on her successful college lecture tours.

In his twilight years, Whit had much to reflect on and be proud of. His television series was nearly the oldest still in syndication, second only to *I Love Lucy*, and he really <u>was</u> a guiding force and creator in the comic book field.

Patricia Ellsworth Wilson:

> *"Well, professionally, he 'made' D.C. Comics. He was hired as the creative head in 1940 and he hired and trained every writer and artist who worked there. For 14 years, he was the guiding star."*

Jane Ellsworth:

> *"He was very proud of the fact that he had a good relationship with the artists and the writers. He thought highly of himself for having such a great group, and he tried to treat them right, because he felt that was all to the good of the whole company. He was very interested in the company itself. He was pleased that D.C. Comics flourished into the 1970's."*

Fredrick Whitney Ellsworth passed away in Westlake Village, California, on September 7, 1980. His vision, his commitment to the best quality possible, and his dedication to all aspects of his career in the various entertainment fields he worked in, is the legacy of a man of much sensitivity, humor...and <u>class</u> -- Mr. Whitney Ellsworth.

Christmas card drawn by Whit, 1969...

...and 1979

...faster than the speediest jet...

...more powerful than the mightiest rocket...

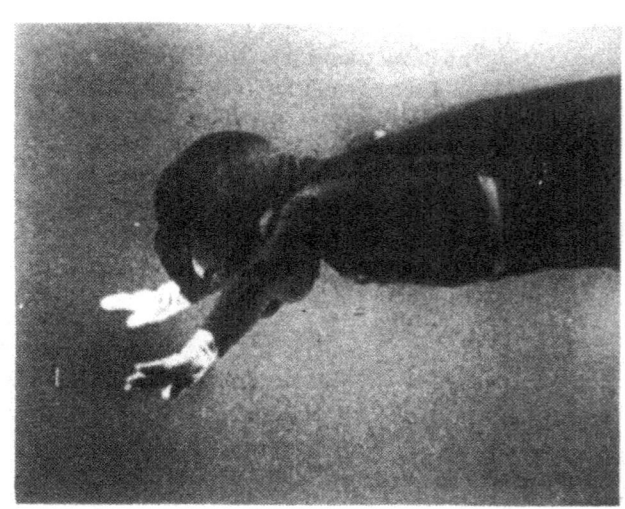

...able to fly around the world faster than you can say SUPERPUP!

Chapter 2

THE ADVENTURES OF SUPERPUP

by Whitney Ellsworth
and Cal Howard
(1958)

novelization by Chuck Harter

...that's Superpup! And only you and I know that Superup is really Bark Bent, star reporter for the Daily bugle. Wow!

The silence in Bent's office was broken by the bumping and squawking of the intercom. Monty Mouse appeared from his sleeping drawer in Bark Bent's desk and exclaimed, "Gee whiz, why doesn't somebody answer this thing?" As if on cue, Bark entered. The excited mouse turned to him and said, "Bark! Grab the intercom, will ya?"

Bark, preoccupied as usual, replied, "Huh?"

"The intercom, can't you hear it?" asked the frazzled mouse.

Bark pressed a switch on the intercom and said, "What is it, Chief?"

Editor Terry Bite's voice howled over the intercom and demanded, "Get in my office right away!" "Okay, Chief," replied Bark who then hurried toward the Editor's office.

Monty Mouse yelled, "Goody, goody, goody, goody, goody," for he knew an angry Terry Bite meant that a story was about to pop. He also knew he wouldn't hear from Bark for a while so he hung his Do Not Disturb sign over the edge of his drawer, closed it and settled down for a nap.

Terry Bite was on the phone as usual, but this time he was really angry. "Madam, I can't help it if the newsboy throws your paper on the roof!" he yelled and slammed down the phone in disgust. "Trouble, trouble, trouble!" When Bark entered, followed by fellow reporter Pamela Poodle, Terry walked over to the edge of his desk and snapped, "Why don't you answer when I call you?" Bark, indicating the hall outside, replied, "I was just, uh...uh."

The gruff editor said, "never mind about that. You panic too easily." He then threw back his head and laughed, "Ha, ha, ha!" Addressing the two reporters, Bite explained, "I just want to tell you what a fine job I think you and Pamela did in helping the police put Professor Sheepdip in jail."

"We could never have done it without the help of Superpup," gushed Pamela Poodle. Bark turned modestly to her and uttered, "Oh, it was nothing." Pamela indignantly replied, "Why are you taking the bows? To think, you're no Superpup!" Bark looked embarrassed and countered, "Uh, me?...Well, anyway, it'll be a long time before Professor Sheepdip gets out of jail." "You're so right, you're so right," agreed the editor. The three newshounds then gathered around a Daily Bugle newspaper, whose headline blazed PROF. SHEEPDIP IN JAIL, accompanied by a photo of the mad scientist behind bars.

Professor Sheepdip was in a cell, but he wasn't sad. In fact, as he held the bars, he began giggling to himself and said, "That's what they think!" He then began cutting through one of the bars with a saw which he had concealed about his person.

Sergeant Beagle was on duty at his jail desk and was whiling away the time by cutting out paper doll figures. He heard the sawing and looked up. Figuring that the sounds

SUPERBOY & SUPERPUP - THE LOST VIDEOS

As the noise persisted, Beagle lifted his left ear to better judge the origin of the sounds.

"They can't get away from the long arm of the law," exclaimed the officer.

The white smoke from the blast cleared, and the good sergeant emerged flattened and dazed.

Professor Sheepdip walked up to the road sign that read TO THE CITY.

He turned it in the opposite direction to reveal THEY WENT THAT WAY written on the other side.

THE ADVENTURES OF SUPERPUP

were only mice, the good sergeant continued to work at his paper figures. As the noise persisted, Beagle lifted his left ear to better judge the origin of the sounds and triumphantly pulled his paper apart to reveal six perfectly cut figures. Hearing a loud crash coming from the direction of the Professor's cell, he questioned in his odd Anglo accent, "What's that? What's that?" and hurried to investigate.

At the back door of the jail, Wolfingham, Professor Sheepdip's zoot-suited sidekick, a.k.a. Sheepdip's Dupe, was fumbling with some skeleton keys. The Professor yelled, "Hurry up, you blundering nincompoop!"

"Uh, I'm tryin' Boss," responded Wolfie as he continued to fumble with the keys.

"Snap out of it. Find the right key," demanded the Professor.

"Duh. The right key," squawked Sheepdip's Dupe, "What am I doin'? Where's the key? Here's a key."

Sergeant Beagle ran up to the Professor's cell, and ignoring the cut bars in his haste, used his pass key and entered. "The blighter's gone!" he exclaimed, and leapt into the air in dismay.

Meanwhile, at the back of the jailhouse, Professor Sheepdip was urging his sidekick, "Hurry up. Will you *please* hurry up and give me the right key and let's get out of here."

"That's the one. That's the key. I told you I'd find it, Boss," replied Wolfingham as he opened the door and freed the mad scientist.

"Where is the getaway car?" inquired the professor.

"Right over dere, Boss," Wolfie indicated as they ran past a police wagon toward the car.

Sergeant Beagle, realizing that his prisoner had escaped, raced from the cell in hot pursuit of the two villains who were speeding away into the desert in their 1958 Chrysler Imperial, laughing hysterically all the while.

The good sergeant, arriving at the back of the jailhouse, called to the fleeing baddies, "I say there. Stop!" When he found this produced no response, he re-entered the jail and emerged with a small cannon. "They can't get away from the long arm of the law," exclaimed the officer, whereby he placed the cannon in position, took aim and fired.

As the white smoke from the blast cleared, the good sergeant emerged flattened and dazed by the force of the cannon's firing.

The shell exploded mere inches from Professor Sheepdip's and the Dupe's Imperial as it sped away.

"Missed us, Boss," sneered Wolfie.

The lawdog collected himself and raced to his custom police wagon in pursuit of the villains who were now almost out of sight.

The wagon, unfortunately, would not turn over. Beagle emerged from the cab and gave the hood a few whacks with his nightstick. This caused the motor to start. The fearless lawman then took off after the scoundrels.

As they continued into the desert, the mad professor and his Dupe came to a sign at a crossroad and stopped.

Professor Sheepdip walked up to the pointed road sign that read TO THE CITY. He turned it in the opposite direction to reveal THEY WENT THAT WAY written on the other side. He then re-entered the auto and left quickly with Wolfingham at the wheel.

Sergeant Beagle, fooled by the change, went in the direction of the misleading THEY WENT THAT WAY sign, clanging the alarm bell.

"You sure are smart, Boss," chuckled Wolfie as the two continued their speedy escape through the desert.

"Yes. We got clean away," agreed the professor.

Montmorency Mouse woke up from his dream. He felt that the story was picking up. "Meanwhile, back in Terry Bite's office..." mused the little mouse.

There was tension in the office of the Daily Bugle editor as he paced back and forth on top of his desk. Bark and Pamela were also concerned about Professor Sheepdip's escape from jail. Sergeant Beagle, fraught with worry, clamored, "I just can't understand it. I was hot on their trail and all of a sudden, they just vanished." Terry replied, "With Professor Sheepdip on the loose again, he'll certainly be looking for revenge." The anxious flatfoot alibied, "What do you expect me to do about it? I did the very best I could."

"Well, what _can_ we do?" asked the editor.

"Easiest thing in the world," explained Bark. "We'll just capture him and throw him back in jail."

"Oh, as easy as all that," taunted Pamela, "You must think _you're_ Superpup!"

"Who, me?" shrugged Barked with feigned innocence.

"I certainly wish Superpup would help us again," said Sergeant Beagle.

"Don't count on that. But I'd give a pretty penny to know what Professor Sheepdip is up to right this minute," countered Terry Bite.

In his laboratory, which he was renting from a certain Professor Pepperwinkle, the mad Sheepdip was busy mixing

SUPERBOY & SUPERPUP - THE LOST VIDEOS

He dipped a paper airplane into the smoking beaker...

..."Come, I will give you a small demonstration of its deadly powers," beckoned Professor Sheepdip to the perplexed Wolfingham...

...an explosion, remarkably similar to the 1950's atomic bomb newsreels, occurred!

THE ADVENTURES OF SUPERPUP

chemical fluids, while Wolfingham looked on with fascination. "What's cookin' Boss, soup?" asked Wolfie as he stuck his finger in the beaker and brought it to his mouth for a taste.

The professor slapped his arm and said, "Get your finger out of there! You want to blow up ze place?"

"Sorry. It tastes awful," complained the Dupe.

"It is worse than it tastes. With this little concoction, we shall get revenge on the Daily Bugle, Mr. Bark Bent and his friends," said the professor, thereupon bursting into maniacal laughter.

He then dipped a paper airplane into the smoking beaker, and went to the nearest window with the Dupe in tow.

"Come, I will give you a small demonstration of its deadly powers," beckoned Professor Sheepdip to the perplexed Wolfingham. He tossed the paper airplane out of the window and watched with smug satisfaction as an explosion, remarkably similar to the 1950's atomic bomb newsreels, occurred.

As they both reeled back from the explosion's impact, Wolfie snarled with alarming perception, "Wow! That was a BIG one!"

Shaking hands in triumph with his sidekick, Professor Sheepdip explained that, "This was just a small idea of what is going to happen to the Daily Bugle building." He then raced over to the lab table and began adding a strange looking liquid to his beaker of explosive formula.

"Whatcha doin' now, Boss?" inquired the dim Dupe. "Why ya pourin' all that stuff in the bottle? Huh?"

"You will see, you will see," answered the scientist, as he attached a fuse to his bottle of volatile mixture. "I want you to take this bottle and go to the Daily Bugle office, and when you get there, light de fuse and blow up the building," he demanded of his loyal assistant.

"Blow up de building?" yiped Wolfie. "Gee whiz, Boss!"

With that feeble protest aside, the professor shoved the hapless dupe into a grandfather clock that just happened to be in the lab.

"Get in zere. Get in ze clock!" ordered the madman. "Here is the bottle and do just what I told you."

"What about me?" cried the frightened Wolfingham.

"We'll worry about that later. Now get going," reassured the professor as he slammed the clock's front door on the forlorn Wolfie.

Suddenly the clock began moving because the learned criminal had cunningly removed its bottom so that his loyal assistant could "walk" to the Daily Bugle.

"Over here, over here," cautioned the evil scientist as he groped toward the door leading out of the lab, for he was still seeing blue dots from the paper airplane's explosion. After Sheepdip opened the door, he narrowly avoided being bumped by the walking clock, and said, "No! This way, you clumsy lummox!"

As Wolfie trotted out into the desert, the mad Professor Sheepdip leapt up and down in happy anticipation of the Daily Bugle being blown to bits! He laughed and laughed and laughed!

Meanwhile, Bark Bent was huddled over his desk, writing a story, when Montmorency opened up his drawer, jumped up and said, "Look! Will you quit leaving your half eaten sandwiches in the drawer? They attract mice!"

"Sorry, pal," apologized Bark.

"What are you going to do about recapturing Professor Sheepdip?" questioned Monty.

"I wish I knew," sighed Bark. "I've got to find him, but I don't know where to start looking."

"Why don't you look in the Yellow Pages?" smirked the little mouse sarcastically.

That did it. Bark had had enough. He pushed Monty down into his drawer and shut it at once.

At the same time, Wolfie suddenly exited the elevator at the sixth floor of the Daily Bugle.

In his office, Terry Bite asked, "What's new, Beagle?" of the morose sergeant, as the grandfather clock subtly entered.

"Well, Professor Sheepdip and his villainous henchman shall not escape the long arm of the law," promised Sergeant Beagle.

"I certainly hope you're right," replied the editor. As the concerned lawman turned to leave, he bumped into the approaching clock, but never having been very interested in grandfather clocks, he took no notice and merely uttered, "Oh, I beg your pardon," and left the office.

Sitting at his desk, the editor gave his watch a cursory look and called out to no one in particular, "What time is it?" The Dupe muttered, "The time? The time is exactly..." and answered the editor by turning the clock's hands to read four-thirty.

"Thank you," said Bite, returning his attention to his work.

SUPERBOY & SUPERPUP - THE LOST VIDEOS

Terry sat bolt upright with popping eyes and shouted, "WHAT!?!"

"This looks like a job for Superpup!" announced Bark as he removed his glasses and left his desk chair.

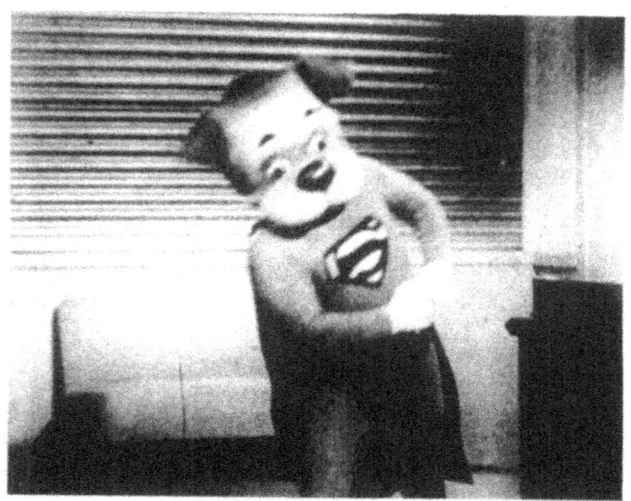

Abruptly, Superpup appeared, and with an exit stage right, rushed to Terry Bite's aid.

Knowing that seconds counted, the Pup Of Steel burst through a wall of the editor's office.

THE ADVENTURES OF SUPERPUP

From inside the clock, Wolfie began making his move and muttered in frustration, "Where are the matches? I know I've got matches. I've <u>always</u> got matches! How can I light it without matches? No matches!" He then opened the front of the clock, exposing his face, and the bomb, and matter-of-factly asked the preoccupied editor, "Excuse me, sir. Do you have a match?"

Bite threw down his pencil in disgust and said, "Oh, interruptions, interruptions. Always interruptions!" He then picked up his lighter and lit the bomb's fuse.

"Thank you, kind sir," replied Wolfie as he re-closed the front of the grandfather clock. The Dupe could be heard to exclaim, "I hope this works out all right. I hope, I hope, I hope!"

"Two and two makes four," mumbled the chief as he huddled over his paperwork. Suddenly, he was struck with the notion of what he had just done. Terry sat bolt upright with popping eyes and shouted, "WHAT!?!" He quickly reached for his intercom switch, pounded his fist on the table and demanded, "Bark Bent, Bark Bent, Bark Bent, Bark Bent!..."

In Bent's office, Monty Mouse opened his sleeping drawer and grabbed Bark's feet, which were perched on the desk. He yelled, "Wake up! The Chief's callin' ya! Wake up! Why don't you get on the ball?"

Bark woke with a start, sat up, pushed the intercom switch and said, "What's up, Chief?"

"Hurry up, I got a bomb in here! Hurry up!" bellowed the frightened editor.

"This looks like a job for <u>Superpup</u>!" announced Bark as he removed his glasses and left his desk chair.

"Goody, goody, goody, goody, goody," squealed the little mouse in happy anticipation of the action to come. "Oh boy! This is GREAT! Wow!" he cheered.

Abruptly, Superpup appeared, and with an exit stage right sweep, he rushed to Terry Bite's aid. Knowing that seconds counted, the Pup Of Steel burst through a wall of the editor's office.

"The bomb! The Bomb! Hurry up! Come on, get it out of here!" yelled Terry Bite to Superpup as he approached the terrified editor. The Krypton Canine, reacting quickly to the imminent danger, grabbed the nearby intercom, went to the nearest window, and tossed it out.

"No, not that!" screamed the frantic news dog in exasperation. "Stop!" His words were spoken in vain as Superpup grabbed the desk's paper, in- and out-boxes, and hurled <u>them</u> out of the window. "Not the papers, you idiot!" barked Terry. The editor then began a tug of war with Superpup over the desk phone, and pleaded, "No, not the phone! The clock! Get it out of here! Hurry up, hurry up, hurry up!"

Superpup raced to the clock and, grabbing it in his mighty paws, leapt into the sky and soared over the city.

Meanwhile, back at Professor Sheepdip's lab, he sighed contently and mixed his evil potions, preparing for further mayhem. Hearing the sound of wind rustling from Superpup's approaching flight, the professor looked up from his labors and said, "What's that?" He then went to his front door, opened it and stepped out onto his front porch. Gazing up, he saw Superpup flying with the clock containing his own Wolfingham.

Wolfie, in fact, had just opened the door and quivered, "You can't do this to me. I want to go home." He looked up at Superpup, who asked, "Where do you live?"

"Twenty-three and a half Rock Gulch," he replied.

"Okay. I'll drop you off," said Superpup, being the helpful hero he was.

"Drop me off? What does he mean by that?" wondered Wolfie as he pulled the clock's door shut.

SUPERBOY & SUPERPUP - THE LOST VIDEOS

Professor Sheepdip jumped up in shock and surprise as Superpup hurled the grandfather clock down towards him. As he cowered near a wall, the clock landed on top of him with a loud explosion.

Superpup flew triumphantly over the city of Pupopolis and returned to the Daily Bugle, blissfully unaware of his temporary victory over the mad professor.

Sheepdip and Wolfie emerged from the smoldering wreckage of the clock and swayed back and forth muttering, "What happened? Where are we?"

Back in Bark Bent's desk, Monty Mouse pondered, "Meanwhile, in Terry Bite's office..."

Pamela Poodle rubbed the newly repaired wall of Bite's office, remarking, "There, everything is back in order again."

"Where is that Bark Bent? He's never around when I want him, and I want him RIGHT NOW! Where is he, where is he?" barked the impatient editor.

"I don't know where he is," expressed reporter Poodle.

"Nobody knows anything around here. Never saw anything like it. Gotta do everything by myself. Oh, I wish I could get some decent help around here," complained the feisty news hound as he returned to his desk.

After Pamela left the editor's office, Superpup made a graceful landing through Bite's office window. Moving quickly and silently past the engrossed chief, he left the office, quietly shutting the door.

"What was that?" Terry reacted looking up, but not fast enough to see the Krypton Canine slip out of his office.

Superpup dashed down the hall and quickly entered Bark Bent's office. Monty Mouse, seeing Superpup return, exclaimed with joy, "He got back, huh? Everything's all right, huh? Oh boy! Goody!"

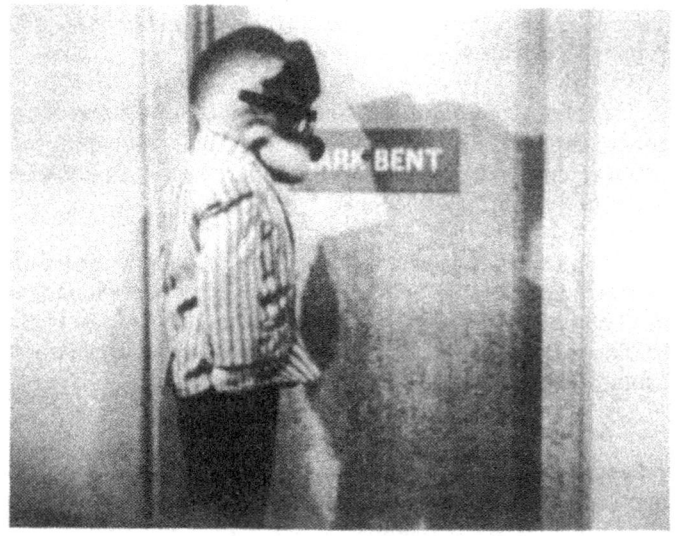

Quickly changing to his secret identity of Bark Bent, Superpup left the office to confront Terry Bite.

THE ADVENTURES OF SUPERPUP

"Where's that Bark Bent?" growled the angry editor as Bark entered the office.

"You called me, Chief?" answered Bark.

"I wish I could get some decent help around here," muttered the chief. "Where were you when Professor Sheepdip tried to blow up the building?"

"Well, I was...uh...," alibied Bark.

"First thing you know, he'll be trying it again," worried Terry.

"Not much chance of that, Chief," said Bark.

Back in Sheepdip's rented laboratory, which had been previously occupied by Professor Pepperwinkle, the mad professor chuckled again, "That is what he thinks!" Reaching for the phone, he said, "Get me the Daily Bugle. I want to talk to Miss Pamela Poodle."

In the Bugle building, the girl reporter responded to the ringing phone with a cheery, "Hello."

Cleverly disguising his voice to that of a society dowager, the professor said, "Hello. This is Mrs. Gotrocks. I'm having a little tea party this afternoon. Twenty-three and a half Rock Gulch. I would like to have you come and cover it for the Daily Bugle."

"I'd love to! I'll look forward to seeing you there," said the newspup.

Professor Sheepdip and Wolfingham, in their lab, prepared to move their rocket outdoors for launching.

Pamela then left her office and soon entered the office of Bark Bent. She said quickly, "Bark. I've just been invited to..." and realized that Bent was not there.

"Bark's not here. Any messages?" asked Monty Mouse from his drawer in the desk. For besides sleeping there, he also took messages for Bark.

"Tell him I'm going to go out and cover a big society party at the house of Mrs. Gotrocks," said Pamela.

"Okay," replied Montmorency Mouse.

Pamela quickly entered her 1957 Austin Healy 2000 and zoomed across the desert toward twenty-three and a half Rock Gulch.

The spunky girl reporter soon reached her destination and striding with confidence, went up to the house and knocked on the front door.

She was immediately pulled inside by Wolfingham.

"Let go of me! Let go of me!" she cried in terror.

"Welcome to the tea party, Miss Poodle," smirked the mad professor.

"Get me out of here!" she begged, as the two villains

SUPERBOY & SUPERPUP - THE LOST VIDEOS

chuckled conspiratorially to each other.

Bark entered his office and asked the little mouse, "Uh, any messages, Montmorency?"

"Yeah. Pamela said she's going to cover a tea party at Mrs. Gotrock's home, at twenty-three and a half Rock Gulch," informed the wee assistant.

"That's impossible," replied Bark. "I happen to know that Mrs. Gotrocks is spending the season at her villa on the French Riviera."

"What!?!" exclaimed Monty.

"This looks like another job for Superpup," said Bark. "Call Sergeant Beagle and tell him to get out there right away!" Monty reached for the phone as Bark headed for the familiar storeroom.

The whoosh of Superpup's flight echoed throughout the Daily Bugle as the lawman came on the line and said to Monty, "Sergeant Beagle here. Hello! Hello!"

Suddenly, because most of the radios in the Daily Bugle were tuned to the same station, and to the delight of all concerned, the William Tell Overture filled the air with its exciting tones. Superpup flew over the tall buildings of Pupopolis in a single bound and raced to Pamela Poodle's aid.

"Help! Superpup!" exclaimed the girl, still tied to the rocket. "Oh, please, Superpup!"

The mighty canine's superhearing picked up her cries, and he increased his speed. Seconds counted!

"Now, my proud beauty, you'll be the first one to take a trip to the moon," gloated Professor Sheepdip, as he eyed the rocket's fuse. "We'll fool them Russians, huh, Boss," mused Wolfingham.

Meanwhile, in back of Professor Sheepdip's lab, Pamela Poodle, tied to a rocket, cried, "No! You can't do this!"

Superpup flew even faster toward the sound of Pamela's cries.

The mad Sheepdip knelt and lit the rocket's fuse.

Pamela cried, "Help! Superpup! Superpup, where are you?"

Superpup could finally see Pamela from the air and flew down toward her.

The professor and Wolfie jumped into a different getaway car, in this case a Studebaker, and sped away from the sputtering fuse, laughing all the while.

The Krypton Canine leapt out the office window.

Montmorency Mouse popped up from Bark Bent's drawer and said to his secret invisible friend, "Perhaps you're wondering why Professor Sheepdip and Wolfingham are using a different car this time. Well, this is gonna be a rough ride and they didn't wanta wreck the new car." Monty then went back to sleep in the drawer for he knew it was just a

THE ADVENTURES OF SUPERPUP

matter of moments before the Pup Of Steel would once again save the day. Superpup soon landed near the rocket.

"Oh, Superpup, am I glad to see you," breathed Pamela in relief as he removed her bonds...

...and led her to safety behind some large rocks.

With a roar, the rocket took off, and as Superpup and Pamela watched, it streaked into the sky.

"Oh, look," said the mighty hero, pointing to the rocket.

"It's chasing them," observed Pamela. Superpup and the girl eyed each other in astonishment as the rocket slowly began a downward turn and headed right for the fleeing heavies.

Inside the car, the professor and his dupe were giggling maniacally, blissfully unaware of their impending comeuppance, mere moments away. As the villains' Studebaker raced through the hills, the rocket headed straight for it. Hearing its roar, Professor Sheepdip turned around in his seat and saw the approaching projectile. "Look! Look what is coming!" he yelled to the oblivious Wolfie.

The missile headed closer.

"Faster, faster, it is gaining on us! Faster!" cried the mad professor.

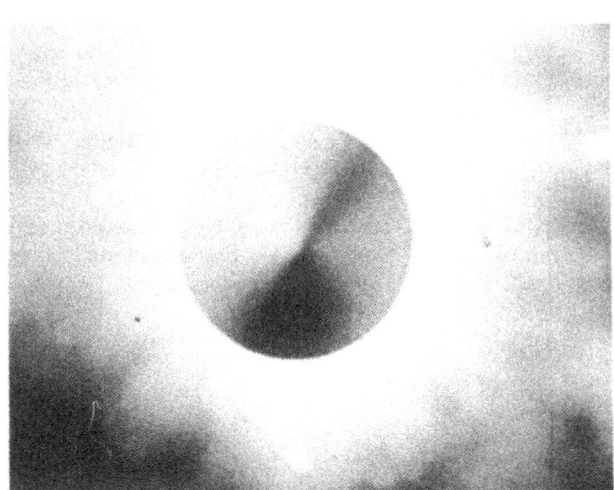

The rocket was almost upon them.

With a fiery explosion, the blast forced the criminals' car off the edge of the road where it tumbled down an incline and exploded on impact.

Moments later, Superpup landed and immediately grabbed both villains and held them, for Sergeant Beagle's police wagon was pulling up alongside. The good sergeant quickly exited his wagon and took charge of the bad guys from Superpup, proclaiming, "Aha! I told you I'd get you! You can't escape the long arm of the law."

Editor Terry Bite and Pamela Poodle hurried out of the wagon and witnessed the arrest. As Sheepdip and Wolfie grudgingly entered the familiar police wagon, a great sense of relief fell over the feisty editor and his girl reporter as they looked happily upon the Super Dog with admiration and respect.

SUPERBOY & SUPERPUP - THE LOST VIDEOS

The canine population of Pupopolis slept a little better that evening, knowing that Professor Sheepdip and Wolfie were once again safely behind bars. They also knew that the following day and every day, Superpup, the Pup Of Steel, would be flying on patrol to insure that Truth, Justice and the American Way were upheld.

Superpup gave the A-OK sign. He knew his work was done, for Professor Sheepdip and Wolfingham were now safely in the noble lawdog's custody.

Leaping into the air, the Krypton Canine flew toward the Daily Bugle building, for Bark Bent had a story to write.

Pamela Poodle watched Superpup disappear into the clouds and sighed, "Ah...isn't he wonderful?"

Back in Bark's office, Montmorency Mouse popped up from his drawer and, thankful for his home and his job, said to his secret friend, "Of course he's wonderful. Everybody knows Superpup is wonderful."

THE END

THE ADVENTURES OF SUPERPUP

SUPERBOY & SUPERPUP - THE LOST VIDEOS

Billy Curtis ("Superpup") meets "Superman" on the ZIV lot.
(Press photo), May 28, 1957

Chapter 3

THE MAKING OF SUPERPUP

"'SUPERMAN' TO RESUME

'Superman' telefilm series goes into production Sept. 23 for its seventh year under Kellogg Co. national sponsorship, with producer Whitney Ellsworth launching the first of 13 new stanzas at ZIV Studios. Phil Ford directs the initial pair. Noel Neill, Jack Larson, John Hamilton and Bob Shayne head the cast of regulars."

(*The Hollywood Reporter*, Thursday, September 19th, 1957)

As *The Adventures Of Superman* series began filming the sixth and ultimately final season, the cast and crew could happily reflect on the fact that the show had become established as one of the most popular children's series of the era. The program, which had been in production since 1951 and had aired for five seasons, had proven to be a complete success with increased ratings as the years went by. Under the guiding hand of producer Whitney Ellsworth, "Superman" had achieved much in the way of quality despite having to operate from the beginning within limited budgets. In fact, when Whit took over the producer's chair in 1953 from first season head Robert Maxwell, he suddenly found himself in the awkward position of having to constantly request that the New York office of National Comics send the production budget on schedule.

Whit's wife, Jane Ellsworth, recently remembered:

"Bob Maxwell said to Whit, "You'll always have to call them (the home office in New York) every week for the money." Whit said, "You're joking! You mean I won't have money for the payroll?" Bob said, "That's right," and laughed. We couldn't believe it! But sure enough, that's the way it was. He'd have to call New York for the money, and they'd complain it was so much. I've come to think it was a kind of game. Nevertheless, Whit was always worried about staying on budget."

It is to Whit's everlasting credit that he was able to persuade the home office to increase the budget so that the last four seasons could be lensed in color. In a unique example of corporate vision, National Comics supported Whit's decision. This combined foresight proved a major factor in the show's continued popularity in syndication after the first color episodes were broadcast in 1965.

During the seasons of 1954 through 1957, "Superman" had filmed 13 episodes per year over a period of two and a half to three months. In order to accommodate such a swift schedule, several shows would be shot concurrently to utilize the same sets and costumes. The cost per episode was approximately $50,000. The total budget for the entire series' run had amounted to $3.5 million, which in these days of skyrocketing television costs, seems almost quaint by comparison.

"3-1/2 MIL 'SUPERMAN' PRODUCTION OUTLAY OVER SEVEN YEARS

With shooting on "Superman" telepix series starting seventh year, Superman outfit has spent total of $3,500,000 in production costs, averaging $500,000 a year, according to exec producer Whitney Ellsworth. Shooting is currently underway at ZIV Studios...Kellogg and Sweets Co. of America co-sponsor on ABC-TV."

(*Variety*, October 13, 1957)

So great, in fact, was "Superman's" increasing success that for the final season, the production had moved from syndication to a major network, ABC-TV.

"'SUPERMAN' SLOTTED ON ABC

Final details have set for the shift of "Superman" to the ABC-TV network where it will air Mondays at 5 p.m. in all zones, with Sweets Co. becoming alternate sponsor this season with Kellogg Co. in the seventh year of the syndicated series."

(*The Hollywood Reporter*, Monday, September 23, 1957)

The show, which was based on the characters appearing in the Superman comic books, had featured the regular cast members of George Reeves (Superman/Clark Kent), Jack Larson (Jimmy Olsen), Noel Neill (Lois Lane), John Hamilton (Perry White) and Robert Shayne (Inspector Henderson). Their fine ensemble acting enhanced every

SUPERBOY & SUPERPUP - THE LOST VIDEOS

George Reeves in "The Superman Silver Mine," 1957

THE MAKING OF SUPERPUP

show and had many times compensated for low budget lensing and some contrived scripts. George Reeves and Jack Larson were so popular that they both had stamped portrait cards printed to answer the increasing deluge of mail from children requesting "autographed" photos.

The "Superman" production company had worked at such studios as RKO-Pathe (1951), California Studios (1953-1954) and the Chaplin Studio in 1955 during its history. [NOTE: No filming was done in 1952.] However, for the 1956 season, and the final season of 1957, the episodes were lensed at ZIV Studios. Television historian Ronnie James recalled this pioneer of TV production:

> "ZIV started out as a radio company. They pioneered the distribution of radio shows on transcription discs as opposed to the network live feats. After several years of success in the radio field, they went into television in 1948. They started producing on film for first-run syndication. ZIV was a pioneer in shooting in color. "The Cisco Kid," "Boston Blackie" and "Favorite Story" were all shot in 16mm color. Later shows of the mid-1950's included "Highway Patrol" and "Men Into Space." ZIV shot a lot outdoors as opposed to being studio-bound. They had a much more invigorating look and atmosphere than many network shows (of the time) which were pretty much studio-bound. ZIV was located at the the old Eagle-Lion Studio on Santa Monica Boulevard just west of the Goldwyn Studios which later was changed to a different name."

During "Superman's" last season at ZIV, George Reeves was enjoying his greatest period of popularity. He was continuing to make personal appearances in the roles of both Clark Kent and Superman, as he had done since 1953. From August to early September of 1957, George Reeves, Noel Neill and a full cast of musicians and entertainers undertook an extensive tour of the state fairs throughout the country. These shows featured both Reeves and Neill in singing capacities, as well as a wrestling match between "Superman" and a costumed villain, "Mr. Kryptonite." The performances, with few exceptions, were well attended with some audiences numbering as high as 50,000. The tour concluded shortly before the last season resumed filming.

The 1957 season's efforts included such shows as *Divide and Conquer*, in which the Man of Steel finds the ability to split into dual Super-men, *The Mysterious Cube*, a crime story in which Superman outwits some crooks by altering a clock, to foil their statute of limitations, *The Superman Silver Mine*, wherein the invulnerable hero magnetizes an iron bar to capture a crook with a metal plate in his head, and *Superman's Wife*, a human interest story in which he stages a fake wedding to capture the villains. For George Reeves, the last three episodes of the 1957 season held a particular interest. Reeves had recently received his membership card from the Director's Guild of America:

> "GEO. REEVES TO DIRECT 3 'SUPERMAN' VIDPIX
>
> George Reeves, star of "Superman" telepix series since its inception, will step into the ranks of star-director next week, to helm three "Superman" stanzas. While this will be Reeves' telefilm debut as a director, he has staged legit producing at Pasadena Playhouse and Newport Beach Little Theatre."
>
> (Variety, Tuesday, Oct. 22, 1957)

Director George Reeves on the set of "The Perils Of Superman," 1957

Reeves' directorial efforts, the last three episodes of the series, included *The Brainy Burro*, set in Latin America and featuring Reeves' personal friend Natividad Vacio, *The Perils Of Superman*, a lighthearted spoof of cliffhanger serials, and the final episode, *All That Glitters*, which featured Phillips Tead in his recurring role as the eccentric scientist, Professor Pepperwinkle. *The Adventures Of*

SUPERBOY & SUPERPUP - THE LOST VIDEOS

The characters of "The Adventures Of Superman" ... and their canine counterparts on "The Adventures Of Superpup"

Noel Neill (Lois Lane) and George Reeves (Superman) hold the September 17-24, 1955 issue of TV Guide on the set of "The Unlucky Number" episode of "The Adventures Of Superman"
Photo courtesy of the John Field Collection

Ruth Delfino as Reporter Pamela Poodle, and Billy Curtis as Superpup, in "The Adventures Of Superpup"

John Hamilton as Daily Planet Editor Perry White in "The Adventures Of Superman"

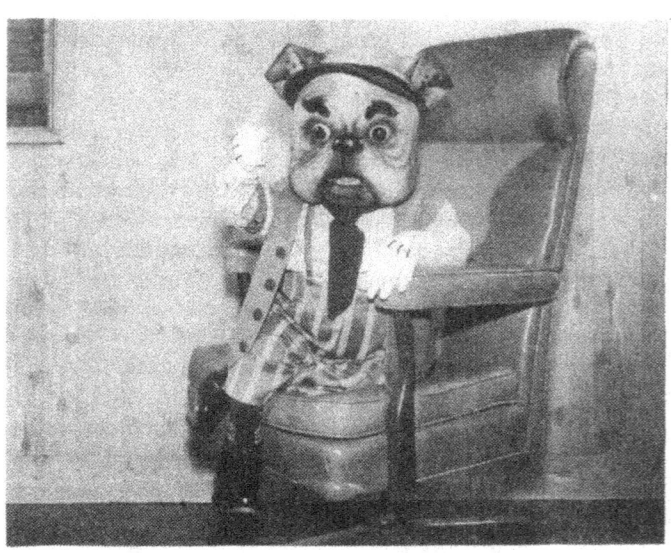

Angelo Rossitto as Daily Bugle Editor Terry Bite [in the same chair being occupied by Perry White (left)]

THE MAKING OF SUPERPUP

Superman had produced a total of 104 episodes, as well as a special short made for United States Savings Bonds, entitled *Stamp Day For Superman*.

The series had been one of the most popular children's shows of the 1950's, and would go on to become a genuine American television classic. As of 1991, the program is still telecast in many markets and is the second oldest series still in syndication after the perennial favorite, *I Love Lucy*.

In 1957, Whit Ellsworth had conceived a spin-off from his popular "Superman" series that would be geared to the very young children's Saturday morning television market. He contacted Cal Howard, who was a Walt Disney cartoonist and had created the early television series, *Broadway Open House*, with Jerry Lester and Dagmar. This late night show became the prototype for the later *Tonight* show. Cal remembers:

> *"He (Whit) was doing Superman and he got this idea that maybe we could do one for kids with animals. He brought it up and I said okay and tried to help him. I said, "I'll do it on spec and if it sells, I'll get some money."*

Whit's idea was to produce a lighthearted parody of the "Superman" series utilizing midgets wearing dog masks. The concept was one of a live cartoon. The series' regular characters were to have been Superpup (the Dog Of Steel), Bark Bent (Superpup's secret identity), reporter Pamela Poodle, Daily Bugle editor Terry Bite, and representing the forces of law and order, Sergeant Beagle. There was an additional regular who was portrayed by a hand puppet and would serve as a narrator, Montmorency Mouse.

The conception of Superpup/Bark Bent, Pamela Poodle and Terry Bite were clearly modeled after their human counterparts from the "Superman" series. Strangely, there was no indication of using a Jimmy Olsen type, based on the character portrayed by Jack Larson. It is not known why the Jimmy Olsen likeness was omitted. The Sergeant Beagle character bears no similarity to "Superman's" Inspector Henderson. Patricia Ellsworth Wilson comments on her father's reasoning toward the "Superpup" pilot:

> *"My father had always enjoyed making children's cartoons. He had a whimsical, funny approach. He thought, because he liked dogs and had a dog, that it would be fun to have the story of Superman set in the dog world. He thought he could have something pretty adorable and delightful for children."*

Whit and Cal Howard collaborated and wrote a script for the proposed pilot entitled *The Adventures Of Superpup*. The plot concerned the efforts of an evil scientist, Professor Sheepdip, and his sidekick Wolfingham to wreak havoc upon the city of Pupopolis. Bark Bent, Pamela Poodle and Terry Bite would work for that great metropolitan newspaper, The Daily Bugle. Montmorency Mouse would live in Bark Bent's desk and would periodically comment on the ensuing action. Once the script was completed, Cal contacted the firm of Allen-Shaw to have some design work done on the masks that the actors would wear. Allen-Shaw was a company that designed toys, architecture, and had done some work in motion pictures and early television. Mel Shaw remembers:

> *"Bob Allen and myself had designed and built the Howdy Doody puppet. Cal had co-written the script (for "Superpup") and recommended us to make the masks."*

Drawings were submitted to Whit, who approved them, and Allen-Shaw began to work on constructing the headpieces for the pilot.

Mel Shaw:

> *"They gave us an advance of $1,500 with the full amount of $5,000 to be paid upon completion of the work. We had about a month or so. The original masks were made out of papier mache with the finished products constructed of fiberglass."*

Although some of the masks' mouths could slightly open and close, there was not much movement permitted by the fiberglass masks. Allen-Shaw's concept, which was not used due to the modest budget of the pilot, had included the use of additional puppet masks of each character that <u>could</u> show the mouths moving while they spoke.

Mel Shaw:

> *"We had suggested making a large mask, and then, for cut-ins, we suggested making hand puppet heads that would be the same, only smaller, that could be animated by hand."*

Unfortunately, this novel approach was not used in the finished print of the pilot.

Mel Shaw:

> *"They didn't want to do it because they wanted an experimental picture first, and if it worked, then they were going to do that."*

The masks each weighed two or three pounds, and when completed, were fitted to the actors.

Mel Shaw:

> *"They fit on the shoulders. We went down

to Western Costume when they were building the costumes and fitted the masks around the necks of each costume. They were made similarly to what ended up in Disneyland for *their* characters."

On the ZIV lot, several technicians on the crew were notified that since it appeared that the "Superman" series was not going to be renewed, a pilot would be filmed at the end of shooting the last episode, *All That Glitters*, with the hope of continuing the crew and sets on a new series. Cinematographer Joe Biroc, A.S.C., who had worked extensively in the motion picture field and had served as director of photography on the 1955 and 1957 seasons of "Superman," was among the first told.

Joe Biroc:

> "At the end of the last season, they said we were going to have some time. We're gonna make a pilot. The main idea was to use the same crew and sets that were still standing at the end of "Superman's" filming in order to save money."

A close examination of the *All That Glitters* episode reveals that with the exception of a few exteriors, all sets used in "Superpup" were nearly, and in some cases, completely identical to those previously seen in "Superman's" last episode. Special effects head Thol "Si" Simonson, who had served in that capacity during the entire run of "Superman," was also told about the pilot.

"Si" Simonson:

> "I heard rumors on it. Finally they decided that this could go...and everybody laughed at the concept. But when they got the characters together, it looked more promising. I'd say the characters developed over a month of time. When they finally got ready to shoot, everybody agreed that they (the characters) were done well, and it was believable, and it was conceivable that they would go."

Production manager, Ben Chapman, who worked on the 1957 season of "Superman," served in the same capacity on the "Superpup" pilot.

Ben Chapman:

> "The approximate budget of "Superpup" was between $25,000 and $30,000. [AUTHOR'S NOTE: This was half the budget of a 1957 "Superman" episode.] It was shot after the "Superman" season wrapped. Whit specified that the show was designed for kids eight years or younger."

Ben also devised a unique way to keep the budget down and to avoid having to overdub the actors' dialogue in a sound studio at a later date.

Ben Chapman:

> "There was no need to lip-sync since the masks' mouths didn't move very much. We seated the voice actors in chairs adjoining the set and they read the dialogue as we shot. It was very simple."

National Comics in New York bankrolled the pilot based on Whit's success with the "Superman" series. Whit's personal belief in "Superpup's" chances caused him to augment the budget with some of his own money.

"Si" Simonson:

> "I remember Whit told me, "I want this done economically, because some of the budget is coming out of my own pocket."

Superpup was shot in color as was the last season of "Superman." Since the lighting, sets and cameras had all been used for the previous season's filming, the use of color photography did not cause the existing budget to escalate. "Superpup" was lensed in color on 35mm film.

Billy Curtis was cast in the dual role of Superpup/Bark Bent. His credits extended back to *The Wizard Of Oz*, as one of the Munchkins. Billy had worked extensively in movies and TV during the 1940's and 1950's. He was featured as a "mole man" in the 1951 Lippert Pictures' feature *Superman And The Mole Men*, starring George Reeves and Phyllis Coates. Billy was no stranger to the "Superman" series' crew and had played the Martian named "Mr. Zero" in the 1956 episode of the same name.

L-R: Billy Curtis, George Reeves, George Barrows and Herburt Vigran in "Mr. Zero," 1956

THE MAKING OF SUPERPUP

Apparently, Billy had quite a dominant personality and left an impression on the people he worked with.

Joe Biroc:

> "I knew Billy Curtis well. I used him a lot as a stand-in for kids. We both smoked cigars. He'd motion me over, pull me down by my tie, and take a cigar from my pocket. He was great to work with. Very nice."

"Si" Simonson:

> "I remember going to Whit's office when Billy Curtis was there. Whit said, "Meet the new Superman." And I said, "Hi, Billy." Whit then said, "What do you think of that?" I said, "Well, I don't know..." because it was hard to visualize at the time. Everybody knew him. Billy was on the ball."

Billy recommended three friends of his, Frank, Sadie and Ruth Delfino, for the respective parts of Sergeant Beagle, Wolfingham and Pamela Poodle.

Frank Delfino:

> "Billy called us and said they needed little people, so you better come up. He was a great person and had a heart for little people. Anytime a job came up, he would call all of us and get us in on the show. He was a very caring person."

Frank Delfino had worked in the motion picture field for a few years and was featured in Paramount's 1956 Danny Kaye musical feature *The Court Jester*. The entire Delfino family had travelled all over the country for the Curtiss Candy Company, and daughter Ruth Delfino had often appeared as the company's trademarked character, "Baby Ruth."

Ruth Delfino Spering:

> "We did a lot of parades and a lot of personal appearance type work."

The Delfinos, as well as the rest of the cast, received a fee of $250 apiece for their work on the "Superpup" pilot.

Angelo Rossitto was cast in the role of editor Terry Bite. He had enjoyed a long career in movies with many credits such as the 1932 MGM horror film *Freaks*. He also appeared in a couple of Bela Lugosi horror films of the 1940's such as *Spooks Run Wild* (1941) and *The Corpse Vanishes* (1942). Angelo played in the 1947 Screen Guild production of *Scared To Death*, also with Lugosi.

"Si" Simonson:

> "I knew Angie Rossitto for years. He sold papers in front of the Warner Brothers Theatre on Hollywood Boulevard. Wonderful person. He was highly regarded in Hollywood."

Rounding out the cast was Harry Monty, who played the part of Professor Sheepdip. Art Weissman, George Reeves' manager and a personal friend of Whit's, manipulated the Montmorency Mouse puppet during the first photo test session.

Art Weissman:

> "My hand puppeteering exploit was a test pattern during the pilot shooting of "Superpup," at which time it was decided to have the mouse pop out of a desk drawer for whatever lines it had to deliver."

Art Weissman manipulates the Montmorency Mouse puppet behind Perry White's chair

The shooting scheduled for "Superpup" was very brief and slightly under the average "Superman" length of four to five days per episode.

Ben Chapman:

> "The shooting was three for four days. You wouldn't dare go over that."

Cal Howard:

> "The shooting schedule was very short. We were short on money and short on time. There was a problem getting the money from the New York office for the "Superpup" pilot. The actors were unable to be kept into overtime and it was a real struggle on Whit's part to get the budget."

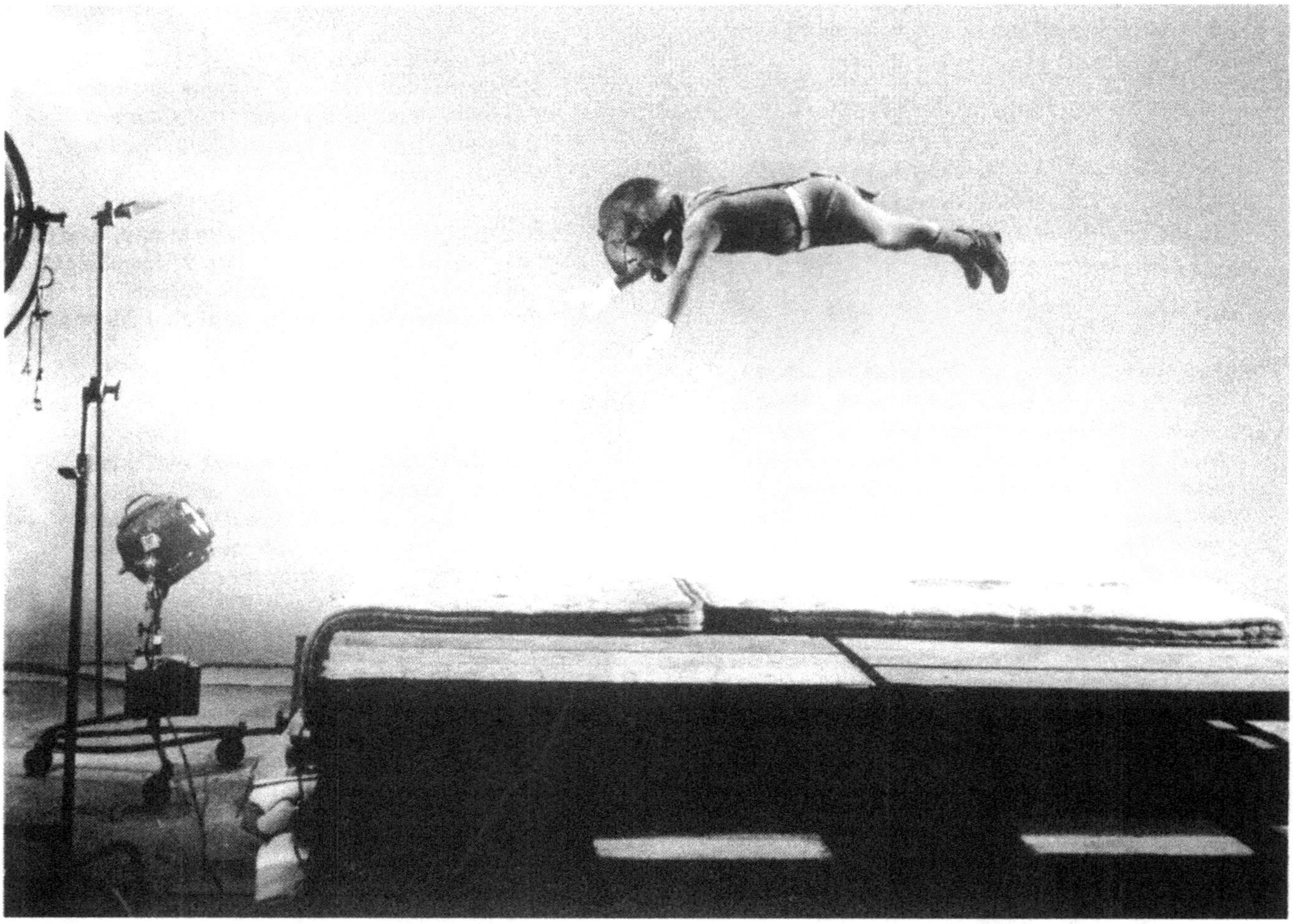

SUPERBOY & SUPERPUP - THE LOST VIDEOS

Billy Curtis balances on the hidden bar during "Superpup"s filming

George Reeves lies on the same bar during the filming of "The Atomic Captive", 1957

THE MAKING OF SUPERPUP

Billy Curtis lies on the grandfather clock that is connected to the hidden pole extending from the background screen. Note technician (far left side) holding a smokepot in front of a fan to simulate cloud movement.

Joe Biroc:

> "The shooting days were eight hours max. It was shot real quick. Whit always had to struggle to get even two dollars more out of the New York office."

Despite the problems with the budget, Whit took the trouble to take care of his cast.

Sadie Delfino:

> "They didn't feed us on the set. Whitney Ellsworth took us all out to lunch. He was very nice."

An amusing incident occurred during shooting when Ruth Delfino (Pamela Poodle) had to drive director Cal Howard's Austin-Healy sportscar.

Ruth Delfino Spering:

> "I had to drive Cal Howard's car. I had to wear glasses to see, but I couldn't get my glasses underneath. So Whit sent me over to Beverly Hills and got me some contact lenses. I've had contact lenses ever since. Whit paid for them out of his own pocket. When I returned, I still had to drive Cal's car. His car was a very special car. He had won all kinds of racing awards with that car and had little medals on the dashboard. He was a little sensitive of my driving. They put bits of wood on the pedals so I could reach them. Somebody rode tucked under the dashboard, just in case."

Cal Howard:

> "I was in the right hand side on the floor. I was shifting the clutch because she couldn't reach. She had to sit up to take the steering wheel. We only went 50 feet or so in the shot."

"Superpup's" flying scenes employed a more simplistic approach than had been used during the 1957 season of "Superman." In three episodes, *The Last Knight*, *The Atomic Captive* and *The Gentle Monster*, new flying scenes had to be shot to supplement the existing stock footage due to plot demands. These brief inserts were not as effective as the previous season's flying effects.

George Reeves was placed on a narrow bar that extended from a pole hidden behind a backdrop screen that was not used for any back projection work. He was suspended approximately five feet in the air over some mattresses that were lying on a two foot platform that was 12 feet long. An off-screen smokepot in front of a small fan created the illusion of flight through the clouds and light gauge thread was used to cause Superman's cape to flutter in the "wind."

Reeves' earlier body plate which he had lain upon had been worn under his costume, and was not used due to efforts of the new appointed production manager, Ben Chapman, to work within the limited budget. Instead, Superman would lie on top of a narrow bar that stretched from his chest to mid-thighs. This device was used for the brief shooting of the new flying scenes. Since the bar did not extend to Reeves' ankles, unlike the previous apparatus which supported his feet, his legs were not as perpendicular as the previous scenes.

Hence, the flying scene in *The Gentle Monster* only shows Reeves' full body for a split second. In *The Last Knight*, the new flying scene takes place in front of a blacked out screen to simulate night. Unfortunately, in *The Atomic Captive*, the bar can been seen as Reeves rolls back and forth on top of it. It is just as well that these scenes are only one or two seconds long, because the defects are not readily noticeable in their brevity.

"Si" Simonson:

> "Ben Chapman took over. He was a very good production manager. He's a hurry up guy. I said, "I need George for a half hour to get him in the body plate..." that would go under his costume. This is how we usually did it. Ben didn't go for that and said to lay a bar on the extended pole instead of attaching the body plate and to put Reeves on that. Ben said not to shoot George full figure since his legs were hanging down due to lack of support. So there are only the quickest of full figure shots in the new flying scenes. It was elementary and, although we accomplished everything we needed, it wasn't quite as good."

When the time came to shoot "Superpup's" flying scenes, this same economical approach was used. Billy Curtis either lay on top of the narrow bar or laid on top of a grandfather clock that was attached to the pole. Frank and Ruth Delfino were both present during the filming of Billy's flying scenes.

Frank Delfino:

> "He (Billy) had to balance himself on the bar. It was seven inches wide. He was laying on that. I would say it was two inches thick."

Ruth Delfino Spering:

> "I remember when he was flying...that they

THE MAKING OF SUPERPUP

had to teach him how to do that because none of us had ever seen that before. It wasn't easy. He had to be pretty strong to hold his legs up. The bar was quite narrow and flat. It was just as long as his torso."

The entire shoot went very smoothly and efficiently with one humorous exception that involved Pamela Poodle.

Ruth Delfino Spering:

"I remember when they put me on the rocket, I kept sliding down, and they had to figure out a way to keep me up there. When I'd struggle, I'd start slipping down! They rigged up a small piece of wood for me to brace my feet against."

When the company finished filming, the raw footage was assembled into a final cut. In an attempt to interest potential sponsors, a space was included in the opening credits for future advertising footage and an announcer recorded the line, "Your product, the best of its kind in the world, presents...Superpup!" If the pilot had been underwritten by the current "Superman" sponsor, Kelloggs, this would not have been necessary. Although the pilot was shot in color, the final cut was printed in black and white to keep within the budget. At this time, the "Superman" episodes shot in color were printed and telecast in black and white. (See CHAPTER 1 - MR. WHITNEY ELLSWORTH.) Everyone involved with the project was happy with the outcome and had high hopes that the "Superpup" pilot would be sold for an upcoming series.

"Si" Simonson:

"I went up to the ZIV projection booth and saw the rushes and final print of "Superpup," and I thought it was good."

Frank Delfino:

"Whit, Cal and crew liked the story, liked the acting, and liked the people. They were very hopeful that in the near future it would be picked up. We had every indication that it was going to air."

Ruth Delfino Spering:

"They were delighted with it. Whit had so much confidence in that thing. He was sure it was going to be a winner."

So positive was the general attitude of the cast and crew toward "Superpup's" potential success, that on November 27, 1957, Whit's 50th birthday, he was presented in his office with a cake that read "To Super Pop." The top of the cake featured a Superman figure made of icing who utilized puppet strings to manipulate a dog villain (not seen in the final print), Superpup and Sergeant Beagle. (See color page, number 48.)

Sometime after this, there was an attempt to hold a preview to interest potential West Coast sponsors and to judge audience reaction.

Cal Howard:

"We took it to a local theater and ran it with us and the rest of the people present. Whit called some other people from the studio. It was stuck in with no announcement. There was a standard audience there and we got permission from the theater operator."

The fact that the black and white print was shown instead of a color one may have contributed to the audience's mild reaction. If the previous feature had been a wide screen color film then the black and white "Superpup" wouldn't have had as strong an impact as a color version.

Cal Howard:

"It was a lukewarm reaction. They watched it and probably looked at each other afterwards."

The copyright date on the print of "Superpup" is 1958. This was probably due to the fact that the new 1957 "Superman" episodes were not broadcast on the ABC network until February of 1958.

Ronnie James:

"For the first several months, the fall of '57 going into '58, the "Superman" re-runs that ran on ABC were the same ones that had been in syndication for some time. Always in black and white. In February of 1958, they started running the thirteen first-run shows on ABC that they shot in '57."

"Superpup" carried the 1958 copyright date possibly since the plan may have been to continue seeking sponsors while the thirteen episodes from 1957 were being first-run on ABC.

In early 1958, Whit sent a print of the pilot to the New York offices of National Comics who would ultimately make the final decision whether or not to keep pursuing sponsors.

Frank Delfino:

"Once we were done shooting, that was the end of it. Whit had sent it back to New York for National Comics to look at. We tried to keep up with Whitney to ask him,

SUPERBOY & SUPERPUP - THE LOST VIDEOS

The Cast Of "The Adventures Of Superpup..."

Billy Curtis as ... SUPERPUP

THE MAKING OF SUPERPUP

... and ... BARK BENT

SUPERBOY & SUPERPUP - THE LOST VIDEOS

Ruth Delfino as ... PAMELA POODLE

THE MAKING OF SUPERPUP

Angelo Rossitto as ... TERRY BITE

SUPERBOY & SUPERPUP - THE LOST VIDEOS

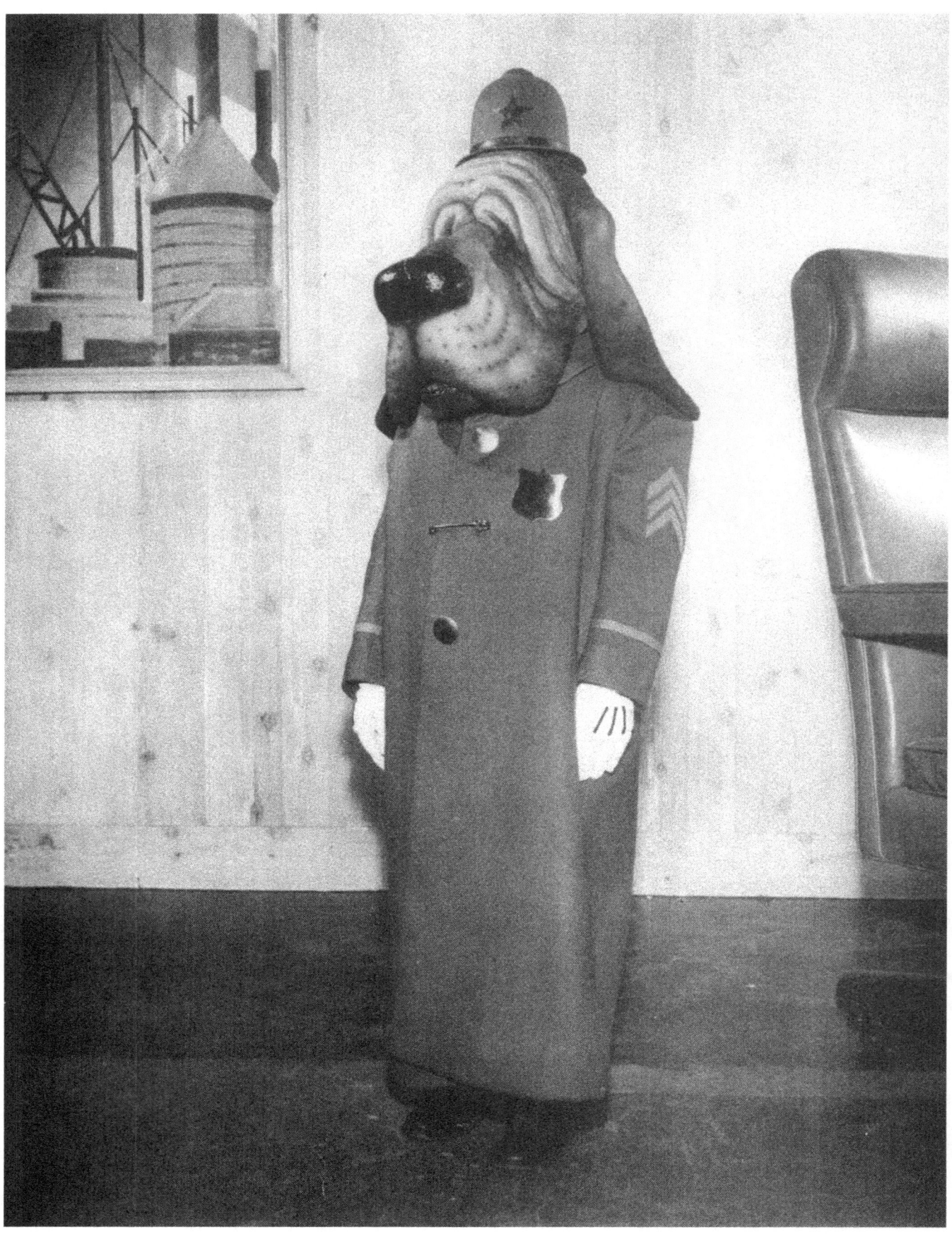

Frank Delfino as ... SERGEANT BEAGLE

THE MAKING OF SUPERPUP

Harry Monty as ... PROFESSOR SHEEPDIP

SUPERBOY & SUPERPUP - THE LOST VIDEOS

Sadie Delfino as ... WOLFINGHAM

THE MAKING OF SUPERPUP

... and Montmorency Mouse as ... HIMSELF

but he said, "It's in New York. They've got it, but they're not doing anything with it." That's all we heard."

"Si" Simonson:

"It was just waiting. Hopeful...trying to get syndication, trying to get this, trying to get that."

The waiting period extended for quite some time. By mid-1958, there was still no definite answer from the New York office.

Ruth Delfino Spering:

"We lived in San Diego. After the shooting...I was young and interested...and every now and then I had to go back to L.A. to have my contact lenses checked. I went back every two or three weeks for several months. I would always stop in and see Whit, and he was always so nice. He always took me around the studio and visited with me in his office. He said, "They haven't done anything with it yet." I think he himself was hopeful. Even if they were stalling. I guess he didn't want to hurt our feelings. He was such a nice guy that he wouldn't want us to lose hope."

Frank Delfino:

"I don't think we ever got the word that it was definitely off. It just petered out. We never got a definite no on it."

The deciding factor that may have contributed to National's ultimate rejection could have been based on economic factors.

"Si" Simonson:

"We never officially heard that it had been rejected. We figured that the rejection happened because they couldn't produce it for the figure they had hoped they'd be able to get it at. They didn't think that it was competitive or they couldn't do enough of them at the right price. That's the kind of feeling I got. I think the people that did it, did it for less than nothing, and the next one couldn't be done for the same figure."

To further reflect, it may have been that National was not really interested in a spin-off from "Superman," but became involved out of their respect for Whit and "Superman's" success.

Frank Delfino:

"I think they (National) were not that interested in it. They just did it because Whitney wanted to do it."

Joe Biroc:

"National didn't put up enough money, they didn't care to push it. They really didn't care."

Ben Chapman:

"National bankrolled the pilot due to Whit's success with the "Superman" series."

The "Superpup" pilot was eventually forgotten, and by early 1961, Whit was preparing to film a pilot for a proposed live action TV series entitled, "The Adventures Of Superboy." (See **CHAPTER 5 - THE PRODUCTION OF SUPERBOY**.)

In retrospect, it is a shame that "Superpup" was not sold and the proposed series never occurred. It was surely a unique attempt at something different in children's television programming and could have become a cult favorite of the genre. Although puppets had been popular on early 1950's TV (with Howdy Doody being incredibly successful) "Superpup" was one of the first times that human actors were combined with animal masks to create the illusion of a human cartoon, in the medium of television for an entire half-hour show.

In 1965, eight years after "Superpup's" demise, a cartoon series appeared on the NBC network that featured a dog superhero. *Underdog*, who's voice was portrayed by Wally Cox, was an immediate success and enjoyed a respectful run. Although the series was quite disimilar to "Superpup," the concept of a dog superhero had proven to be a valid and successful one.

By the 1970's, most of the people involved with "Superpup" had forgotten all about the project. None of the actors had ever seen a complete print since they lived on the West Coast and the only print that was struck from the original negative was in New York at the offices of D.C. Comics. Frank Delfino became the "Hamburglar" for *McDonald's Restaurants* in 1970, and continues in the part to this day.

Over the years, there was very little written on the 'Superpup" pilot, with *Movie Monsters* Vol. 1, No. 2, February 1975, and *Fantastic Films*, June 1978, being the only magazines to have coverage of the pilot. References in both publications were brief and only one photo was printed. (It showed Superpup and Pamela Poodle hiding from the rocket's take-off.) There was a mention of the pilot in the book entitled *Superman! Serial To Cereal*, written by Gary Grossman, and published by Popular Library's "Big Apple

Books." Unfortunately, the reference was very short.

This was the sum total of journalistic coverage of this "lost" fantasy video from the early days of television.

By the mid-1980's, memorabilia conventions held in areas like civic halls, had become quite popular and frequent. These events, in which such nostalgic items of popular culture from the past are bought and sold, have grown to be a country-wide network of collectors.

It was at several of these conventions that VHS videotapes of "Superpup" and its companion pilot, "Superboy" began appearing. The source of the prints was not known, but both pilots were in black and white and were of exceptional quality.

In preparing the manuscript for this book, the author screened one of these prints for all of the people that were interviewed. Many had never seen a print, and the rest had not seen it for over 30 years.

The responses were for the most part positive and nearly universal.

Jane Ellsworth:

"I liked it. I did feel though, at the very beginning of it that I didn't like it as well as I did as it went on. I thought it was very cute."

Patricia Ellsworth Wilson:

"I think the idea was very good, and I think there are moments in the pilot that really take off, where it's really kind of zany and wildly funny, particularly around the things that the mad scientist does."

"Si" Simonson:

"My wife and I liked "Superpup," and we thought it was entertaining, and kids today would like it."

Ben Chapman:

"It was all right. We did the best we could.

Cal Howard:

"We did our best and I believe we got a lot out of what we had to work with. After seeing it again, we should have been able to take our time and planned the thing more, but that wasn't possible."

Joe Biroc:

"It was funny. That poodle gal was so damn cute."

Frank Delfino:

"I really enjoyed it. It's a shame that it didn't happen. But maybe New York didn't have the foresight that Whitney did. I think that today's kids would like it. It's unique even now. Way ahead of its time."

Sadie Delfino:

"It was fun. I believe that kids would like to see it."

Ruth Delfino Spering:

"Marvelous. Adorable. I was delighted to see it again. After all these years, the thoughts had faded, and seeing it again just brought back a rush of happy memories."

With the current incredible success of the *Teenage Mutant Ninja Turtles* films, the concept of human actors portraying animals has proven to be a valid one. Ahead of its time, and unique of its time, *The Adventures Of Superpup* will be remembered as a novel and entertaining interpretation of the Superman legend.

Original Credits ...

THE MAKING OF SUPERPUP

SUPERBOY & SUPERPUP - THE LOST VIDEOS

Four scenes from "The Adventures Of Superpup."

THE MAKING OF SUPERPUP

Polly Poodle and the Pup of Steel share a tender moment during "The Adventures of Superpup."

SUPERBOY & SUPERPUP - THE LOST VIDEOS

George Reeves lies on the "flying" bar in the "Superman" episode "The Atomic Captive," 1957.

A thrilling scene from "The Adventures of Superpup."

Whit Ellsworth celebrating his 50th birthday in his office on the ZIV lot, November 27, 1957. (Note cake reads "To Super Pop")

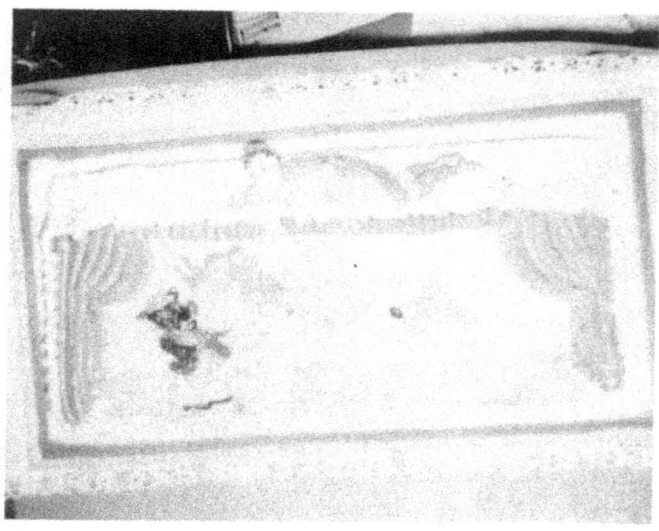

Close-up of the "Super Pop" cake with an icing "Superman" manipulating three characters from "The Adventures Of Superpup."

THE ADVENTURES OF SUPERBOY - "RAJAH'S RANSOM"

Superboy!
It's the Adventures of Superboy!
Incredible boy of Steel; powerful, fearless, invulnerable.

Only survivor of the doomed planet Krypton, home of a race of fine and noble humans far advanced over those of our own world.

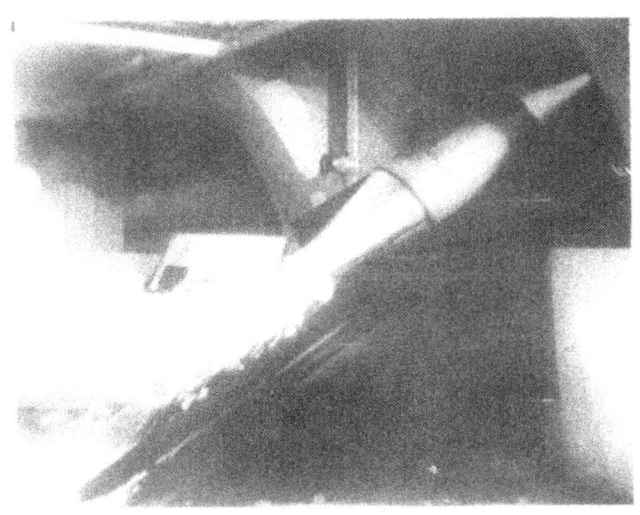

Superboy, whose scientist father sent him hurtling into the far reaches of interstellar space in a tiny craft moments before the great Krypton exploded into a billion billion fragments.

SUPERBOY & SUPERPUP - THE LOST VIDEOS

Speeding the spaceship unerringly in its course for planet Earth...

...where landing safely, the infant Superboy was found and adopted by a small town couple, Jonathan and Martha Kent.

And now, some years later, the child is young Clark Kent, a student at Smallville High School, where his meek, retiring manner hides an exciting secret known only to himself and his foster parents. The secret that Clark Kent is, in reality...

Superboy, champion of the oppressed, enemy of evildoers, dedicated to the cause of truth and justice.

Chapter 4

THE ADVENTURES OF SUPERBOY
"RAJAH'S RANSOM"

by Vernon E. Clark
and Whitney Ellsworth
(1961)

novelization by Chuck Harter

It was a sunny weekday afternoon in Smallville High School. In Miss Gibson's classroom, Donna Givney was addressing her classmates on the subject of her father's occupation. "...After he completed the filtration plant in India, Father's company sent him to South America to supervise construction of a similar facility there," boasted Donna with obvious admiration. "But Father says he was proudest of the fact that he was in charge of developing the new water system right here in our own hometown of Smallville," she added, not wishing to be too immodest. The rest of the students in the classroom applauded lightly as Donna took her seat.

"That was a very good talk, Donna, and your father certainly has an interesting occupation," commented Miss Gibson favorably. "Thank you," replied Donna as she became seated. The teacher then checked the list of names on her desk for the next student. "Our next speaker on 'My Father's Occupation' will be Jimmie Drake," she announced.

Jimmie, a blond, slender, sensitive-looking boy appeared startled. With great reluctance he approached the front of the class and said apologetically...

"My father is the doorman at the Aero Theatre. Period!"

Looking embarrassed, he ignored the muted giggling of his classmates. Seated next to each other in the rear of the class, Clark Kent and his girlfriend Lana Lang appeared concerned over Jimmie's embarrassment.

"Jimmie, is that all you have to say?" asked Miss Gibson.

"That's all there _is_ to say," replied Jimmie, looking very humiliated. Jimmie felt he had to leave immediately and asked the teacher, "May I be excused, Miss Gibson?"

"Well, time is almost up, anyway," she answered. "Jimmie, we'll take this up again at our next public speaking class. Class dismissed," announced the teacher. Looking neither left nor right, Jimmie rushed ahead of the other students toward the door. Lana felt very concerned for Jimmie. The other kids shouldn't have laughed at his embarrassment. "Let's walk home with him, Clark," she asked her special friend.

"Okay, Lana," Clark replied as they hurried to catch up with Jimmie.

Walking hand-in-hand, the young couple soon overtook the morose youth. "Jimmie! Wait up!" implored Clark as they rushed toward him.

Jimmie spoke first. "I was listening to all of you talking about your fathers' jobs and careers. Well...what can you say about a doorman at the Aero?" he said defiantly. "Jimmie, my father works in a grocery store," reassured Clark. "And my father's just a teacher," said Lana, adding, "I'll bet _your_ father makes more money a year than _mine_ does..."

Jimmie wasn't convinced. "Your father _owns_ the grocery store," he said to Clark. "And _your_ father's a professor," he said to Lana. "They both have standing in the community." It was obvious that this subject had been bothering Jimmie for quite a while.

Jimmie spotted his father exiting the doors of the Aero

Theatre. He was dressed in a turban and exotic clothing to publicize the Aero's current feature, "Rajah's Ransom." "There's Dad now," said Jimmie. "They bought him a new uniform for the premiere. Big deal," the youth muttered in disgust. "See you later," said Jimmie to the pair as he abruptly left for home.

He appreciated Clark and Lana's words of kindness, but he knew they wouldn't change anything. His dad was still only a theater doorman.

"He's certainly being unfair to his father," said Lana to Clark, "What's wrong with being a theater doorman?" "Nothing, Lana, except...you know. He thinks his dad's job doesn't amount to much," said Clark sadly, for he knew Jimmie had been upset about his dad's job for a long time. "Well, Jimmie should consider the man and not the job," commented Lana. "Mr. Drake had to raise Jimmie without even a wife to help him and I think that's a lot more important than installing an old filtration system in South America, don't you?" she questioned, referring to Donna Givney's arrogant speech. Lana didn't even like Donna because she was always bragging.

"Yes, yes I do," agreed a startled Clark. For he had been trying to think of a way to bolster Jimmie's ego.

As the young couple headed toward home they passed three men sitting in a parked car in front of the Aero.

. . .

In the driver's seat, Jake Ferde sat behind the wheel, his brother Gunner next to him. They appeared to be well dressed businessmen. In the back seat, by contrast, the third member of the party, Shifty Barnes, had the look of a criminal type, with rough features and a cheap suit.

Shifty spoke impatiently, "All right, all right. Are we gonna sit around here all day?" to his partners. "Why don't you relax, Shifty?" reassured Jake. "Gunner and I have to pull this job. You don't." "Yeah. You don't mind if we do a little planning, do you?" added Gunner sarcastically. "A two-bit movie house in a two-bit town," said Shifty. "The way you guys talk, you'd think you were gonna take Fort Knox." "You'll think it was Fort Knox when we split up the loot," retorted Jake. Reaching for the ignition, Jake asked his brother, "You seen enough, Gunner?" "Yeah, let's go," replied the cool Gunner.

The villains' Chrysler New Yorker convertible then eased its way into traffic and left the scene. They would be back.

. . .

Jimmie Drake and his dad Fred lived in a small one-room apartment over the Aero Theatre. It was clean but on the shabby side. Jimmie looked sad as he sat at his desk and listlessly attempted to do some homework. Fred Drake, hunched over his drawing board, noticed his son's empty gaze and quietly asked, "What is it, Jimmie?" "What's what, Dad?" the youth replied, still looking distantly.

Fred put down his drawing pencil and approached his son. "Something's wrong. Ever since you got home from school, you've been sighing and staring into space. What happened? Did you fail an exam?" asked the concerned father.

"You know I don't fail exams, Dad," answered Jimmie. "I'm just concentrating," he said, not wishing to tell the reason for his distress. "Well, that's just about the most distracted concentration I've ever seen," said Fred Drake. "Now what happened?" He was determined to find out the source of his son's unhappiness.

"What happened, Jim?" demanded Fred. Jimmie knew he was going to have to tell his father the truth. He turned to him in anguish, "This is going to sound terrible to you, Dad, but we had oral essays in class today about our fathers' occupations, and when my turn came I couldn't find anything to say about you," said Jimmie, hating the hurt he had just inflicted on his dad. Fred's face showed no emotion as he digested Jimmie's explanation, then said, "Well, aside from the costumes he wears, I don't suppose there's much to say about a theater doorman, is there?" After a pause he added, "On the other hand, I make no apologies for being one."

"You know, Jimmie, we can't all be airplane pilots or great surgeons or builders of dams in far off places," Fred explained quietly to the boy. "Background, circumstances, responsibilities...these are factors that put some of us into ordinary jobs for all of our lives," Mr. Drake continued, "So we hope for better things for our sons." Jimmie listened intently and appreciated his dad's straight talk.

"...And Jim, between us, we're going to get you through college and into your chosen profession. Now when that's accomplished, I'll consider myself as successful as anyone you know," reassured Fred, adding, "You know what I'm talking about?" Jimmie smiled a little and answered, "I think so, Dad."

THE ADVENTURES OF SUPERBOY - "RAJAH'S RANSOM"

Fred chuckled and, grateful for a good son, said, "No, you don't, but you will." He then returned to his drawing board, picked up his sketch and said, "Hey Jimmie, come here and look at this." Jimmie walked over to his dad and looked at the sketch. It was a very good likeness of him!

"Now that's not bad for a correspondence school artist, is it?" asked Fred. "You're coming along pretty good, Dad," said Jimmie holding the drawing with pride and delight. Having shown his son the sketch and wishing to lighten the mood, Fred suggested, "Well, that's _my_ homework, now suppose you get back to yours."

Jimmie returned to his schoolwork feeling better about his father.

. . .

In a cheap hotel on the bad side of Smallville, the brothers Ferde watched Shifty Barnes nervously pacing the room. "Why don't you go sit down? Shifty, will you relax?" implored Jake Ferde to his anxious cohort.

"This is gonna be perfect. All you have to do is your part of the job right," said Jake, "Just keep Superboy busy."

"Just keep Superboy busy," replied Shifty sarcastically. He was really nervous.

"I'm the pigeon in this deal. I'm the one who goes to jail," worried Shifty. Gunner spoke to the harried Shifty and said, "For three months, six month at the most. Now, isn't that worth fifty thousand bucks?"

"Besides, Jake and me are takin' the real chances," added Gunner. "Suppose somebody should see us?" He then began combing his hair.

"Suppose they do," quipped Shifty. "Who's gonna know ya? That plastic surgeon guy made you look like a couple of movie stars." Smiling with satisfaction and patting his hair into place, the vain Gunner replied, "Yeah. He _did_ do a good job, didn't he? Mother would never know us." Jake, the leader, checked his watch and said, "You boys stay right here, will ya? I wanna go check on the movie." He then left Gunner to his hair combing and Shifty to his worrying, and headed for the theater.

Jake, sat in his parked car across the street from the Aero Theatre and read the poster board in the lobby:

A REAL RAJAH'S RANSOM!
$200,000 IN GENUINE UNCUT
DIAMONDS EXACTLY AS USED IN
THE FILMING OF THIS GREAT
MOTION PICTURE!

A short distance from the billboard, near the sidewalk, was a display case which contained a small pile of glittering diamonds. Standing behind the case, Mr. Edmond, the Aero Theatre manager and Fred Drake, clad in his costume, admired the sparkling gems.

"Two hundred thousand dollars' worth of diamonds! Smallville has never seen anything like this," boasted Mr. Edmond. Indicating the billboard, Fred Drake observed, "Like it said, a Rajah's ransom."

"What time does the star of the picture get here?" asked the doorman. "Seven-thirty tonight, along with the producer and other studio bigshots," answered the confident manager. "A hometown star and two hundred thousand dollars's worth of diamonds. This picture will do the biggest business in our history."

"Well, I wouldn't want the responsibility for those diamonds," said Fred. As the manager and the doorman headed back into the theater, two armed security guards assumed their posts by the display case of gems.

Jake sped away from the theater to rejoin his cohorts in crime.

. . .

With Jake at the wheel, the three crooks drove to a deserted canyon and stopped. "Why, Shifty, you're nervous," chided Jake to his squirming sidekick. "Wouldn't you be?" answered the worried Shifty.

"Well, you better not be nervous, not while you're shooting that rifle," ordered Jake. "You be sure you hit a tire. You gotta stop him." "I'll stop him, all right, _if_ he shows up," said Shifty.

"Oh, he'll show. He comes by here every day right on schedule. Just like a train," reassured Jake.

"I wish I was on one," replied Shifty with sardonic humor. "There's where you're going," said Gunner, pointing to an isolated shack at the edge of the canyon.

SUPERBOY & SUPERPUP - THE LOST VIDEOS

"Now, go on. Get up there while there's no one around," commanded Jake to his henchman. "Good luck." As Shifty hurried toward the shack with his rifle in tow, Jake and Gunner quickly headed for the Aero Theatre.

Shifty watched them drive away until they were out of sight, then used a skeleton key to enter the shack. He didn't have long to wait, for as Jake had said, the Police Chief's car soon pulled into view.

Taking careful aim, Shifty fired one round from his M-1 carbine and with his usual accuracy, hit a tire on the squad car. As the escaping air let out a squeal, Police Chief Parker pulled to a stop and stepped out of his vehicle.

Shifty fired again, and the Chief instantly took cover behind his car and returned fire. "This is Chief of Police Parker. Stop firing and come out of there," he echoed to the still blasting Shifty. Realizing that he was pinned down, the Chief reached inside the car for his radio microphone and said, "Chief Parker calling Superboy! Chief Parker calling Superboy!"

. . .

In the Kent living room, Clark and Lana were going over some homework while Martha Kent, seated on the couch, attended to her knitting.

"What's wrong with the light?" wondered Lana aloud as she noticed the living room lamp flickering on and off. "I don't know. Maybe it needs a new bulb," answered Clark. "Oh," replied Lana, unaware of the code signal established by Chief Parker and Superboy.

Thinking quickly, Clark said, "We'll finish these math problems later, Lana. I don't feel like doing anymore right now." "You promised me you'd help me with all the problems, Clark," reminded Lana, not noticing the exchange of glances between young Kent and his mother. "Why can't we do them now?"

"Never mind, Lana. You come and help me with the cookies for the church social," offered Martha Kent to the puzzled young girl. "Perhaps when we've finished, Clark will feel like working again."

"Well, when the young genius is in the mood, please notify this eager student," snipped Lana irritably as she rose to join Martha Kent. "Come on, Lana," said Ma Kent as they both adjourned to the kitchen.

After they left, Clark put his pencil down and headed toward the bookcase, which he quickly turned to reveal a secret passageway. As he closed the fake wall behind him, he heard the Chief's voice coming over a ham radio receiver.

"Chief Parker calling Superboy! Chief Parker calling Superboy!"

Turning on the broadcast microphone, Clark answered, "Go ahead, Chief. This is Superboy."

"I'm on the Woolten Road. About three miles west of Smallville. Somebody's blasted my tire with a rifle and has got me pinned down behind the car," responded the Chief.

THE ADVENTURES OF SUPERBOY - "RAJAH'S RANSOM"

"I'm leaving right away," said Clark as he took off his glasses and began changing into his Superboy outfit.

Meanwhile, Lana returned to the living room, and noticing young Kent's absence, said in exasperation, "That boy. Disappeared again," and returned to the kitchen.

By now, Clark had changed into his Superboy costume, and lifting a trapdoor in the floor, jumped into the basement. Superboy ran down a hidden corridor and...

...pushing aside a large boulder which served as a door, entered the countryside. After carefully putting the boulder back in place to conceal the entrance, he leapt into the air and flew in the direction of the Chief. Within moments, Superboy spotted Parker in distress and landed by the stricken squad car.

"Hi, Superboy," said the relieved Chief. "Hi, Chief," replied the Super Teen.

As Shifty fired another couple of rounds, Parker noted, "He's just been keeping me pinned down. I don't think he's even trying to hit me." "I wonder why," said Superboy.

"Well, I don't know. I could have radioed for some of my men instead of for you, but I didn't want anyone hurt," said the thoughtful Chief. "Good. Let's see what I can do with him," said the Boy Of Steel.

"You up there! You better come out," commanded Superboy of the gunman. Shifty responded with yet another round of gunfire.

. . .

Meanwhile, Jake and Gunner approached the Aero Theatre to pull off the heist.

"Now remember, Gunner, after you throw that bomb, don't breathe any of that sleeping gas, and then cover me while I grab the stones," said Jake to his brother. "Right," answered Gunner as he left the car to make his move.

Walking slyly past the two armed guards, the two criminals paused, and as Jake gave the signal, Gunner tossed the gas bomb. The smoking fumes quickly rendered the guards unconscious, whereby they fell to the floor.

Taking a deep breath, Jake smashed the glass case and quickly gathered up the jewels. As he ran to the getaway car, Fred Drake opened the door to the theater. Spotting him, Gunner fired off a round, which fortunately missed. The two crooks then sped away from the scene of the crime.

Once he knew the coast was clear, Fred rushed to aid the downed guards. He too, though, was soon overcome by lingering gas fumes and fell unconscious to the street.

. . .

Back at the canyon, Shifty was still firing in the direction of the Chief and Superboy. "I guess he wants to do it the hard way" said Superboy. "Last chance up there. Are you coming out or am I coming in after you?" This was answered by additional shots from Shifty's rifle.

SUPERBOY & SUPERPUP - THE LOST VIDEOS

As Shifty continued firing, Superboy ran...

...toward the shack...

THE ADVENTURES OF SUPERBOY - "RAJAH'S RANSOM"

...and burst...

SUPERBOY & SUPERPUP - THE LOST VIDEOS

...through the wall.

THE ADVENTURES OF SUPERBOY - "RAJAH'S RANSOM"

The cornered crook fired several times at the Boy Of Steel...

SUPERBOY & SUPERPUP - THE LOST VIDEOS

...and watched in horror as the bullets bounced harmlessly off him.

THE ADVENTURES OF SUPERBOY - "RAJAH'S RANSOM"

As Shifty continued firing, Superboy ran toward the shack and burst through the wall. The cornered crook fired several times point-blank at the Boy Of Steel and watched in horror as the bullets bounced harmlessly off him.

Superboy strode over to Shifty and, taking his rifle, bent the barrel and hurled the weapon to the floor.

Collaring Shifty he said, "Let's go talk to the Chief."

As Superboy and his captured crook approached the squad car, the radio announced, "Chief Parker, from dispatcher. Chief Park, from dispatcher." The Chief reached for the mike and replied, "This is Parker. Go ahead." "Jewel robbery at Smallville theater. Two guards and employee still unconscious. No witnesses so far," advised the voice.

"See if you can seal off the town. I'll be there as quick as I can," Parker instructed the dispatcher.

"Here he is, Chief," said Superboy as he turned Shifty over to the officer.

"Somebody just grabbed the diamond display at the Aero Theatre," announced Parker. "I'll see you later," answered Superboy, leaping into the air. As Superboy flew away Parker said to Shifty, "Now before I put the cuffs on you, let's see how good you are at changing a tire."

While Superboy was speeding toward the theater, Jake and Gunner parked their Chrysler New Yorker in a remote area of Smallville, and changed to a different car. They quickly left the scene in a Plymouth Fury. Superboy landed in front of the Aero as the manager and a policeman helped the guards and Fred to their feet. The effects of the gas were only temporary, and they were coming around.

"Superboy! They took my diamonds, my fabulous display!" cried the traumatized manager. "Did anyone see anything?" questioned Superboy. "The guards were knocked out. They didn't see anything. Nobody saw anything," answered manager Edmond.

"I saw them. Two men in light suits," offered Fred Drake. "Can you describe them any better than that," asked the Boy Of Steel. "They were just average looking. They headed east in a convertible. The license number was PBT595," remembered Fred. Superboy responded, "Thank you," and took to the air in pursuit.

He quickly landed by the abandoned New Yorker and after noticing the license plate and checking the empty interior, took off again back toward the Aero Theatre.

. . .

Meanwhile, in front of the Aero, Fred Drake, now joined by his son, reassured the distraught Mr. Edmond, "Well, at least the diamonds were insured and fortunately none of us was hurt." "It's the display. A world premiere for the first time in our history and we've lost the Rajah's ransom," exclaimed the upset manager. Suddenly Fred, his son and the theater executive heard the sound of Superboy's approach and looked up to see him about to land.

"I found the abandoned car. They evidently switched

SUPERBOY & SUPERPUP - THE LOST VIDEOS

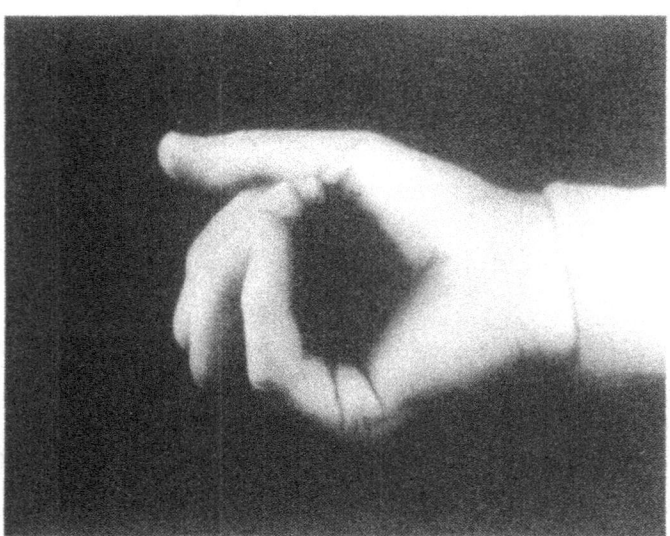

Superboy's hand closed on the coal...

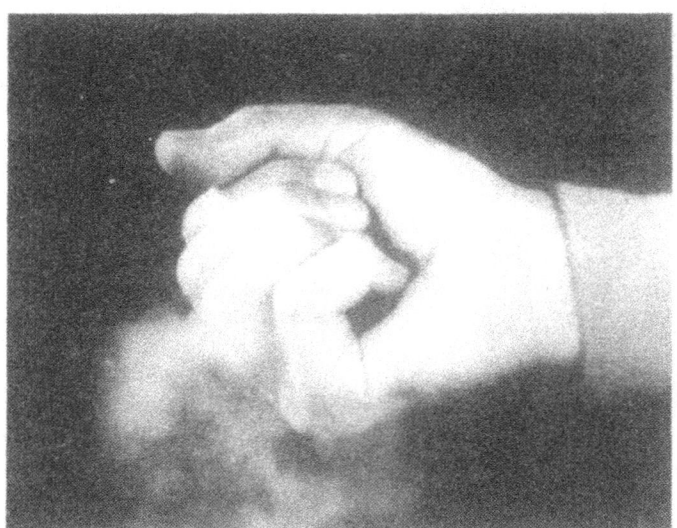

...and after an outpouring of smoke from between his fingers...

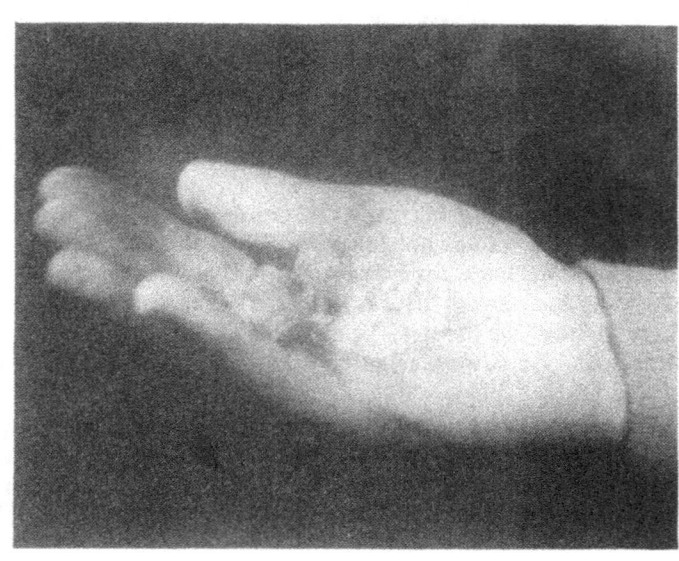

...opened to reveal the glittering jewels.

THE ADVENTURES OF SUPERBOY - "RAJAH'S RANSOM"

and made a complete getaway," spoke the Teen of Steel. "No way of telling which direction they took. Now, my super-vision doesn't do any good unless I know what the men look like. Would you recognize either of them, Mr. Drake?" "Yeah, I'm sure I would," replied the doorman. "Good," said Superboy, "then let's go down to Chief Parker's office and look at some mug shots."

"But what about my diamond display, my premiere?" begged Edmond.

"What kind of heat do you have at police headquarters, Officer?" asked Superboy of a nearby lawman. "Coal furnace, why?" responded the policeman. "I'll send you some pretty fair imitations until we get the real ones back", said Superboy to the manager. "May I go with you, Superboy?" asked Jimmie Drake. "Sure, Jimmie," answered Superboy.

. . .

Superboy, Fred Drake, Jimmie and the officer entered the squad car and headed toward the Police Station. A short time later, Fred Drake found himself looking through a book of mug shots as Chief Parker, Jimmie and Superboy looked on.

"The two men I saw aren't in these books, Chief," offered Fred futilely. "You know, Chief, it can't be a coincidence that Shifty was doing all of that shooting, just at the time the thieves were stealing the diamonds," mused the Boy Hero. "There has to be a connection." "Of course you're right," said the Chief as he began going through the mug shot book. "Wait a minute. Shifty Barnes. Look him up here. Here, we are, known accomplices and partners in most of his crimes are two brothers, Jake and Gunner Ferde," said the Chief as he found the brothers' mug shots.

"You sure those aren't the two men, Fred?" "Positive," answered Drake. "No fingerprints at the scene of the crime, no identification of the criminals. Looks like we're stuck," said Chief Parker.

"You could _draw_ the two men, couldn't you, Dad?" spouted Jimmie. "Yeah, I guess I could," responded Fred Drake. "I didn't know you were an artist, Fred," said Parker. "Well, I'm not an artist...," said Fred humbly. "He is, _too_! He's good! Give him some paper and a pencil, Chief Parker," said Jimmie. Parker said, "Excuse me, Fred," and reached into his desk drawer for the drawing materials.

Superboy motioned to Jimmie to join him on the other side of the office. "That was a great idea, Jimmie, but while your Dad's working on it, will you do me a favor?" Young Jimmie eagerly responded, "Sure, Superboy! What do you want me to do?" "Go down to the furnace room and get me about a dozen pieces of coal." "Coal? What for?" "Remember when I told your Dad's boss I'd do something for him? Well, I don't want to go back on my word. Get the coal, huh, Jim?" said Superboy, giving young Drake an encouraging pat on the shoulder. "Okay," said Jimmie, as he hurried toward the furnace.

Superboy walked over to the desk to observe Fred Drake's drawings. "Say, he's pretty good," uttered the Chief. "He sure is," agreed Superboy. "Our friend with the rifle wouldn't tell you anything when you questioned him, huh?" asked Superboy. "He wouldn't even tell us his name. We had to get his fingerprints to identify him," said the Chief in exasperation. "Would he take a lie detector test?" suggested Superboy. "Not a chance. What's more, he knows that we can't make him take one," answered the Chief.

"Chief, how long do you think he'll go to jail for that stunt he pulled today?" asked the Boy Of Steel. "Oh, three to six months. The worst we can charge him with is malicious mischief and resisting arrest. Unless, of course, we can tie him in with the jewel robbery," answered Parker. "If he _is_ tied in with the jewel robbery, and you can't prove it, three or six months in jail is pretty light for his cut of the diamonds," observed Superboy wryly. "That's right. I'm convinced those are exactly the odds that he's playing for," agreed the Chief, "But proving it is another matter."

At that moment, Jimmie Drake returned from the furnace room. He said, "Superboy," indicating a box of coal he was carrying. "Be right with you, Chief," said Superboy as he accompanied Jimmie to another part of the office. "Thanks, Jimmie," said Superboy. "Sure, but what are you gonna use it for?" asked young Drake. "Just this. As you know from what you've studied in school, diamonds are nothing more or less than pure carbon which has been subjected to tremendous heat and pressure, and of course coal is carbon," explained Superboy, as he grabbed a handful of coal from the box.

"So, I'll subject this piece of coal to super-pressure and in a moment I've created synthetic diamonds. Practically as good as the real thing." Jimmie looked on in wide-eyed astonishment as Superboy's hand closed on the coal and, after an outpouring of smoke from between his fingers, opened to reveal glittering jewels. "Good enough anyway for your Dad's boss and his lobby display, as soon as I've made a few more batches." Superboy repeated the process and produced enough gems to replace those stolen.

Back at the desk, Chief Parker observed of Fred's drawing, "This one's a blond." "No, I just haven't filled it in yet. They both have dark hair. Like this." explained Fred, continuing to draw. "Good, good," observed the Chief. "Well, make it as accurate as you can, it's important."

"There, that ought to do it," said Superboy to Jimmie as he crushed the last of the coal into diamonds. "Now take them down to the theater, Jim." "Sure, but I wanted to wait and see Dad's drawings," said Jimmie. "Later, Jim. These are pretty important to Mr. Edmond," urged Superboy. Jimmie smiled and hurried toward the office door.

"They're excellent drawings, Mr. Drake," Superboy complemented the artist. "They sure are," agreed the Chief. "The point is, do they really look like the two men?" "I'd stake my life on it," said Fred Drake confidently.

"Chief, could you have Shifty Barnes brought in here?" Superboy asked. "Why not?" responded the Chief, who went to his intercom and said, "Have Shifty Barnes brought in here." Then, turning to Superboy, the Chief asked, "Do you think you can really get anything out of him?" "I don't know for sure. But I think I can give him a lie detector test without his even knowing it," said Superboy assuredly. "How?" asked Parker. "Well, as you know, lie detectors work on the simple premise that a subject's pulse steps up in spite of himself if he tells a lie," explained Superboy. The Chief understood. "Sure. I see. You're going to listen to his pulse with your super-hearing." "That's right," answered the Boy Of Steel.

Chief Parker watched Shifty being brought in. "Here he comes." The crook displayed no emotion as he entered the office. Superboy's super-hearing picked up the rhythmic thump of Barnes' pulse. "Do you know anything about the diamond robbery?" asked Superboy bluntly, as he listened to Shifty's pulse quicken. But he remained silent. "Do you know Jake and Gunner Ferde?" The pulse increased even more. "Do you know these two men?" asked Superboy as he showed Shifty Fred Drake's now completed drawings. The pulse now raced at a startlingly quickened pace, and the crook had not spoken one word. Convinced that Shifty was indeed involved in the robbery, Superboy said to Parker, "We don't need him anymore, Chief." "All right. Take him back," ordered Parker, as Shifty was led back to his cell.

"He was in on the diamond robbery. He knows the Ferde brothers," said Superboy. "He recognized them in the sketches." "So, Jake and Gunner had plastic surgery to change their faces," concluded Parker. "Right," said Superboy and addressed Fred Drake. "Now -- would you be willing to be the bait in a trap? Now, it might be very dangerous." "I'll do whatever you say," agreed Drake. "Good," responded Superboy.

"Now, we'll put these sketches on the wire to every newspaper in the country, giving the name and address of the artist, and you must stay in your apartment. Don't go out for any reason." The Chief further explained, "The criminals know they can't be convicted by the sketches alone, but they can be convicted by an eye witness -- the artist who drew the sketches. So, eliminate the artist." Fred Drake looked concerned, but was determined to go through with the plan.

. . .

In their cheap hotel room on the seedy side of Smallville, Jake Ferde was reading the Journal Press. A front page headline read -- **HAVE YOU SEEN THESE MEN?** -- along with Fred Drake's drawings. Gunner kept busy by checking the ammunition in his pistol. "You know these drawings don't mean a thing," said Jake. "It's the guy that made them that's important. We get rid of him, we get rid of all our worries."

Taking the paper, Gunner looked in a mirror and compared his own likeness to that of the drawings. "You're right," said Gunner, "You know, he's pretty good at that. In fact, he's too good for his own good. Where did it say he lives?" "Over the movie house in Smallville," answered Jake.

Gunner reached into a drawer and took out an additional pistol, which he gave to his brother and said, "Let's go back there and pay him a visit." With grim faces, they left the room on their deadly mission.

. . .

Meanwhile, at Smallville High School, Clark Kent, Lana Lang and the rest of the class were engrossed in a mathematics test.

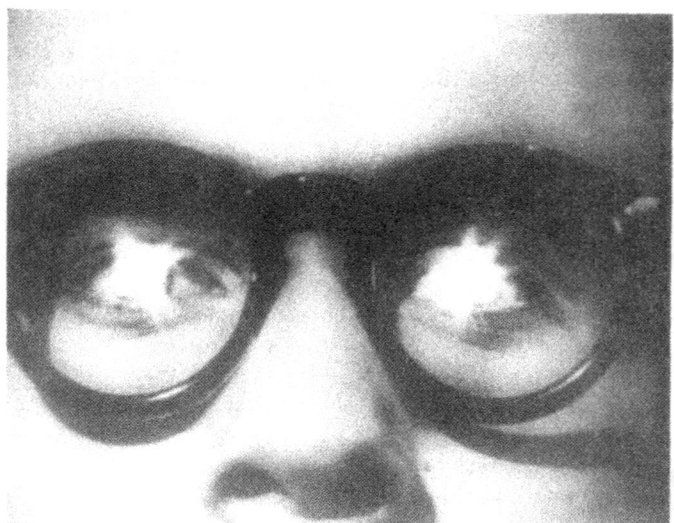

Seated by a window, next to Lana, Clark used his X-ray vision and looked through a wall to observe the Aero Theatre. "You've been looking out that window all morning," noticed Lana and asked, "How come you keep

THE ADVENTURES OF SUPERBOY - "RAJAH'S RANSOM"

Clark knew he had to act fast, so he quickly finished the test...

staring at that old building?" "I wasn't staring at it, Lana. I guess I was staring through it," answered Clark. "You'd better get busy with your math problems," snipped Lana, "Or does the genius just have to guess at the multiple choice answers?"

Their teacher addressed her, "You're not discussing the exam, are you, Lana?" "Well, in a way, yes," answered Lana truthfully, "But we weren't helping each other." "You may be disturbing the others," warned Miss Gibson.

Once again using his X-ray vision, Clark noticed two suspicious looking men were pulling up in their car at the theater. Reaching for a newspaper under his desk, he compared Fred Drake's drawings with the two men. It was them. Clark knew he had to act fast, so he quickly finished the test and approached the teacher's desk. "I'm finished, Miss Gibson, may I be excused?" he requested. "Well, if you think you've checked all the answers, yes," said the teacher. "Thank you," replied Clark as he hurriedly left the classroom, while Lana looked on in amazement.

...and shoved him onto the front seat. The crooks quickly sped away.

. . .

Fred was working on a drawing in his apartment, when the phone rang. He answered, "Hello." Unknown to him, it was Gunner on the line who said, "Hello, Mr. Drake. I'm calling from the emergency hospital. Your son has been injured. Not critically, but can you get over here right away?" "I'll be right there," said Fred as he gathered up his hat and coat.

At that moment, Clark had ducked behind a wall of Smallville High School to change into Superboy.

As Fred Drake left the theater, he was immediately accosted by Gunner, who said, "Hold it. Your kid's all right, but you're not. In the car. Go on!"

Superboy appeared from behind the school building, and once again using his X-ray vision, saw that Fred Drake was no longer in his apartment over the Aero.

As Fred entered the car, Gunner slugged him unconscious with the butt of his pistol...

He instantly leapt into the air.

THE ADVENTURES OF SUPERBOY - "RAJAH'S RANSOM"

Superboy flew even faster and landed in front of Drake, where he stood with his arms folded.

By now, the crooks had reached a deserted road near the edge of Smallville. They pulled to a stop and dragged the unconscious Drake from their car. "Well, he's still out all right," said Gunner. "We'll fix it so he'll stay out for good," replied Jake. "We'll make it look like a clear case of hit and run, with no connection with us or the diamond robbery." They dragged the unfortunate Drake to the middle of the road and dropped him coldly on the ground.

Superboy, having spotted them with his super-vision, increased his speed. The evil brothers backed their car down the road preparing to run over the unconscious Drake.

Superboy flew even faster and landed in front of Drake, where he stood with his arms folded. Advancing in their car, Jake Cried, "Look! There's Superboy!" "Keep goin'! Put it to the floor!" shouted Gunner.

The car sped toward Superboy and crashed soundly into his invincible body, coming quite abruptly to a complete stop.

Superboy turned toward Fred, who was coming around again. "They tricked me. They said they were calling from the emergency hospital," spoke the still-shaken Drake. "That's where they'll be going," answered Superboy, with only a small trace of irony.

. . .

Later, in Chief Parker's office, Fred, Jimmie and Superboy had gathered to hear the outcome of the case. "Fred, the insurance company is rewarding you with a full scholarship for Jimmie, at any college that he wants to attend," announced the pleased Parker. "That's not all. They're offering you a job in their office in Metropolis at maybe more money than you're getting now."

Fred Drake looked at his son. "Well, what do you say, Jim? Should I quit my job and leave Smallville?" "Whatever you decide, Dad. I'm with you," answered young Drake with glowing pride in his father. Fred's decision was that he'd rather stay, and relaying that to Parker he said appreciatively, "Well, tell them no thanks, Chief. I like the people here and I'd like to go on with my art lessons. Who knows...?" he said and shrugged, "Maybe someday..."

Fred turned to the Boy Of Steel and shook his hand. "Superboy, I want to thank you for saving my life." "You're welcome, Mr. Drake," replied the smiling Superhero. "Lots of luck to you, Jimmie," he added and shook the youth's hand. "See you, Chief," Superboy said as he leapt out an office window and flew away.

. . .

The next day, at Smallville High School, in Miss Gibson's class, the first period had begun. "Students, we'll continue today with our public speaking class. Last time we left off with Jimmie Drake. So today, we will start with him. Jimmie..." said the teacher.

In marked contrast to the previous class, Jimmie walked quickly and confidently to the front of the schoolroom and addressed his classmates with terrific pride, "My father is the doorman at the Aero Theatre, but he's the best theater doorman in the United States!"

The class burst into spontaneous applause. Jimmie continued, "...And that isn't all he is. He's a brave man, a kind man, a smart man..."

Clark and Lana exchanged smiles in the back of the classroom, and then returned their attention to Jimmie's speech.

THE END

THE ADVENTURES OF SUPERBOY - "RAJAH'S RANSOM"

SUPERBOY & SUPERPUP - THE LOST VIDEOS

John Rockwell "flies" past light reflectors and crew members on location at Bronson Canyon, Griffith Park, California, 4/4/61

Chapter 5

THE PRODUCTION OF SUPERBOY

Ziv-UA's 'Superboy'

Hollywood, April 18.

Ziv-United Artists has just completed the pilot film for a projected "Superboy" vidpix series. Juve thesp John Rockwell stars as the title character delineating the comic strip fave, Superman, as a youth.

Projected series of half-hour duration is produced by Whitney Ellsworth, primed for syndication. George Blair directed the pilot episode.

Variety, April 19, 1961
(Reprinted with permission of *Variety, Inc.*)

This small announcement in the Hollywood trade publication *Variety*, during the spring of 1961, heralded the arrival of a new production by *The Adventures Of Superman* head, Whitney Ellsworth. In early 1961, he had contacted writer-producer Vernon Clark, who was working at ZIV Studios, to begin co-writing some scripts for a proposed "Superboy" series. Vernon's daughter, Virginia Clark, now an editor at the publishing firm of Simon & Schuster located in New York, recently recalled her father's activities at ZIV.

Virginia Clark:

"My father was a producer of many of ZIV's television shows such as "Highway Patrol," "Rough Riders," and "Harbour Command." Whit and Vernon were close friends."

ZIV cinematographer Dick Rawlings, who would ultimately work on *The Adventures Of Superboy* pilot, also recalled *Rajah's Ransom* co-author, Vernon Clark.

Dick Rawlings:

"Vernon was a writer-producer. He was involved with ZIV from the very start on "Highway Patrol." He was ZIV's head writer."

During early 1961, thirteen scripts were written for the projected "Superboy" series' first season. Whit wrote all of them with three different collaborators. Vernon Clark co-wrote three stories, including *Rajah's Ransom*, *One Man Team*, and *Superboy Vs. Superboy*. Another writer, Paul Harber, co-authored *Superboy's New Parents*, with the remaining nine scripts co-written by Robert Leslie Bellem, who had worked with Whit on several scripts for *The Adventures Of Superman* series. The Superboy character had starred in his own comic book since 1949, and by the late 1950's, had become one of D.C. Comics' better sellers.

An eight page story entitled *The Saddest Boy In Smallville*, appeared in the *Superboy* comic book No. 88, April, 1961. With but a few minor plot differences, this story was nearly identical to the *Rajah's Ransom* script. This same D.C. Comics' publication contained another story called *One Man Team*, which was also quite similar to the unfilmed *Adventures Of Superboy* script of the same name. It is not positively known whether Whit co-wrote these comic book stories, since author credits were not given, but as he was still working for D.C. Comics at the time, it is reasonable to suppose that he did.

Ben Chapman:

"Whit had the thirteen scripts ready so if the series was picked up, they wouldn't waste any time and could go immediately into production. All they needed to do was polish them." (See **Chapter 6** - **The Series That Might Have Been** - **The Twelve Unfilmed "Superboy" Scripts**, for the full details on these proposed stories.)

After the scripts were completed, Whit began to contact several of his previous associates from the "Superman" series to see if they would be available for the pilot's filming. Last season "Superman" production manager Ben Chapman, was notified and agreed to participate.

Ben Chapman:

> "Whit contacted me with this idea for a "Superboy" pilot. I was doing "Flipper" at the time, down in Florida. I became a sort of assistant to Whit and agreed to take a short leave of absence from "Flipper" as a favor to him."

"Superman" special effects head, Thol "Si" Simonson, also agreed to work on the pilot, but in a limited capacity.

"Si" Simonson:

> "I was working on something else and I told Whit I would do what I could. He said, "We're gonna have to do things different. We're gonna have to do it for a price." And if it was tough on "Superpup," it was even more so on this. He wanted the production to be more professional than "Superman" and that was going to be hard to do."

George Blair was signed to direct the pilot. He had worked in that capacity on "Superman" from the 1953 season through the end of the show, with the only exception being the 1955 season, in which he did not participate. Outstanding "Superman" episodes that he had directed included *A Shot In The Dark*, *The Face And The Voice*, *The Clown Who Cried*, and *Perry White's Scoop*, all from 1953. Notable efforts from 1954 included *Olsen's Millions*; *Clark Kent - Outlaw*, *Flight To The North*, and *The Seven Souvenirs*. *Peril In Paris* and *The Phony Alibi* were two strong efforts from 1956 with *The Mysterious Cube* and *The Superman Silver Mine* being effective work from the 1957 season. By 1961, as Whit made preparations for his new pilot, ZIV Studios had undergone a change in ownership. Television historian Ronnie James recalls:

> "In 1959, the year after "Superpup's" demise, ZIV merged with United Artists and had become known as ZIV-UA, Inc. instead of ZIV Television Programs, Inc., which it had been previously called."

From his office on the ZIV-UA lot, Whit announced that auditions for the lead role of "Superboy" would be held. A young actor on the lot named John Rockwell, was soon aware of this upcoming opportunity. A novice to the acting profession, John hadn't acquired much experience, but had studied his craft at various motion picture studios.

John Rockwell:

> "I studied originally with Agnes Moorehead at 20th Century Fox, and then did a "Playhouse 90" show as an extra. Paul Newman was the star, and suggested I go back to New York and study with Sandy Meisner. It just so happened, Sandy came out to see him, and I said, "I want to be in this class." They said, "We're only taking professionals," but I talked my way into the class. And who was in the class...Barbara Rush, John Erickson, Dyan Cannon and Terry Moore...a few people. Before the "Superboy" pilot, I did a few things at ZIV, including "Lockup," with MacDonald Carey. When "Superboy" was casting, I was working on the lot on a pilot called "Time Out For Ginger." I also studied at Warner Brothers. They had an acting school. Ty Hardin and I did a film together called "As Young As You Are" for Paramount."

When John heard about the "Superboy" part being available, the 23 year old actor went to Whit's office to audition.

John Rockwell:

> "I went over and found out where the office was on a break, and said to Whit, "You don't have to look any further. I can fly." I walked in and he was playing gin rummy with the head of the studio. I was a very good gin player at the time, so I said I would play the winner. Whit won, so I started playing him and began winning. So I more or less knew I had the job. I _did_ have to read a few lines, but I _think_ I got the job because I was a good gin player."

John was with GAC (General Artists Corporation) at the time and received a salary of $5,000. Once approved by Whit and his associates, he was cast in the dual role of Clark Kent/Superboy.

"Si" Simonson:

> "I was there when they cast Rockwell and everyone agreed. They liked him. He was really very good."

Jane Ellsworth:

> "I went down to the studio. I thought John Rockwell was very good. I thought he really looked the part."

A short piece of film has survived that apparently was used to test John's makeup in the role of Superboy. Shot in Whit's office, John is briefly interviewed about his sports activities at Warner Brothers. He comes across with a great deal of warmth and charisma, which undoubtedly reaffirmed Whit's decision to cast him. In fact, his ease in front of the camera is surprising for a novice.

THE PRODUCTION OF SUPERBOY

-- JOHN ROCKWELL SCREEN TEST --
(Interviewed/Auditioned by Whitney Ellsworth)

Clapperboard reads S 11.

Technician: The "S," take one.

Whit: Hi.

John: Hello there.

Whit: Is it true that your name is Clark Kent?

John: Yes, but most people here know me as John Rockwell.

Whit: John Rockwell?

John: Yeah.

Whit: You mean John Rockwell is Really Superboy?

John: No, no, no.

Whit: John Rockwell is really Clark Kent and Clark Kent is really Superboy.

John: That's it, that's it.

Whit: I get it. Very confusing indeed. Tell me, John, outside of acting in the medium, as we say in the medium, what do you do? You play basketball for Warner Brothers and that sort of thing, huh?

John: Right. I like sports and I like athletics and waterskiing, swimming, and you know, wrestling...

Whit: But this jazz about playing basketball for Warner Brothers. Why doesn't Warner Brothers put you under contract? If they want you to play basketball, they should send you to college instead of...

John: Well you know something, most people playing for Warner Brothers, they don't even work there. Yeah. There's a couple of people. Well, Ty Hardin for one. He's playing on the basketball team and the other couple of kids that's playing, they don't work there at all. I went to school there, more or less. I guess that's why I'm playing.

Whit: Oh, I see. It's a pretty phony sort of basketball when nobody on the team works for the boss, huh?

John: Well, I guess you could say that.

Whit: We're in on you now in sort of a close up to see how the makeup covers your beard and we're gonna pause now and we're gonna have the camera push right in tight...

John: To a real close-up.

Whit: ...To a real close-up of the third whisker from the left under your eye tooth or something to see what it does there. Okay?

John: All right.

Whit: Right. Cut.

-- END --

For the important role of Clark Kent's girlfriend, Lana Lang, Whit conducted tests with the four finalists who were competing for the part. These screen tests, which have also survived, consisted of on-camera interviews, along with two scenes centered around an electric typewriter (from the unfilmed script *The Box From Krypton*). John Rockwell appeared as Clark Kent and Superboy with each of the four aspirants. The actresses who made the final auditions for the part of Lana Lang were Bunny Henning, Trudy Ellison, Marlo Ryan and Mary Ann Roberts. After the tests were concluded, Trudy Ellison had been cast in the small role of Donna Givney, who would appear at the beginning of *Rajah's Ransom*, and Bunny Henning, an attractive blonde, has been signed for the part of Lana Lang.

Bunny Henning and John Rockwell act out a scene from "The Box From Krypton" in Whit Ellsworth's office.

SUPERBOY & SUPERPUP - THE LOST VIDEOS

From the same test, With John Rockwell now playing the part of "Superboy."

Two of the actors cast as villains in *Rajah's Ransom* had previously worked on the "Superman" series. Richard Reeves, signed to play Shifty Barnes, had appeared as a heavy in the "Superman" episodes, *No Holds Barred* (1951), *Jet Ace* (1953), and *The Big Freeze* (1955). Charles Maxwell, who was cast as Gunner Ferde, had appeared in *The Superman Silver Mine* (1957).

John Rockwell was soon sent to the Western Costume company in Hollywood to be fitted for his Superboy uniform. There, he found the colors of the material to be quite different than what he had expected.

John Rockwell:

"The costume was gray and brown. I couldn't understand why, and they said it photographed better because the pilot was not going to be shot in color. There were two costumes made at the time of the pilot. They were returned to Whit after filming, and I don't know what happened to them. The boots were suede."

From the thirteen scripts that were written prior to the pilot, *Rajah's Ransom* was chosen to be the one filmed. This appears to have been Whit's decision.

Ben Chapman:

"Whit picked "Rajah's Ransom." Everything was his decision."

In retrospect, economic reasons may have been a factor in Whit's decision to use the script that was filmed.

Ronnie James:

"It's quite possible to me that the reason they did the show that they selected was because they wouldn't have to hire and commit to a long-term contractual option, somebody to play Pa Kent. You have to pay actors extra money to tie them up. It's obvious D.C. Comics bankrolled it. The fact that it does not say during the end credits "produced in association with ABC, NBC or CBS" leads me to believe that it probably was produced on spec without a network commitment."

Another possible motivation may have been the fact that a story quite similar to *Rajah's Ransom* had appeared in a *Superboy* comic, and might be previously known to the potential audience. D.C. Comics had taken a definite interest in the production.

Dick Rawlings:

"There was a representative of D.C. Comics overseeing the production."

The shooting time allotted to the pilot was to be very brief, as had been the schedule for the "Superpup" pilot.

John Rockwell:

"It was three to four days, with the flying scenes done the following week."

Dick Rawlings:

"Since it was a half hour show, I would say the shooting time was three to four days. The budget was between $35,000 and $50,000."

Shooting began on April 4, 1961, with location work at the famous Bronson Canyon, located in Griffith Park, California, and the site of much production work at the time.

John Rockwell remembers the crew being concerned that his safety was not endangered.

"When we were on location and I was about to go through the cabin wall, they wanted to make sure I was going through the right one, because they only built one fake wall."

Dick Rawlings:

"The cabin scenes were filmed in Bronson Canyon during a one day shoot. They brought the four walls up there and put them together and built the cabin."

THE PRODUCTION OF SUPERBOY

Preparing for the run. Note production manager Ben Chapman in white short-sleeved shirt. Griffith Park, 4/4/61

SUPERBOY & SUPERPUP - THE LOST VIDEOS

John Rockwell being filmed from the camera car on the road leading to Griffith Park, 4/4/61

THE PRODUCTION OF SUPERBOY

*John Rockwell enjoys a laugh between takes in Griffith Park;
Director George Blair is behind the wheel, 4/4/61*

SUPERBOY & SUPERPUP - THE LOST VIDEOS

John Rockwell, Robert William (Police Chief Parker) and crew, Griffith Park, 4/4/61

THE PRODUCTION OF SUPERBOY

L-R: Director of photography Dick Rawlings, assistant cameraman Harry May, John Rockwell, and an unknown technican on location in Bronson Canyon, 4/4/61

As the filming progressed, John was desirous of reshooting some scenes due to his relative inexperience as an actor.

John Rockwell:

> "We shot a couple of things and I wasn't really happy with the way they came out. I asked if we could reshoot and George Blair said, "No, no. Keep on going. It's okay." I thought I could have done better on some things."

For Superboy's "take-offs," the methods used to propel George Reeves into the air were tried at first, but were soon discarded due to John's natural athletic ability.

John Rockwell:

> "A couple of times they had something for me to spring off of, but it looked phony. So in the end, I just dove over the camera, which had been placed on the ground. I could dive because I used to do a lot of gymnastics."

For his landings, John would simply leap down from a tall ladder that was out of camera range. The optical effects used to depict bullets bouncing from Superboy's chest had been previously employed in the "Superman" series. Animated bullet shells would appear to flatten and ricochet from Superboy's "invulnerable body."

The next day, on April 5, 1961, all of the interiors of the pilot were filmed. These included the Kent home, a Smallville High School classroom, and Chief Parker's office at the Police Station. It is in this scene in Chief Parker's office, that Virginia Clark noticed a comic reference to her father. During the brief moment in which the original mug shots of Jake and Gunner Ferde are displayed on camera, a close examination will reveal that the two villains were arrested by a Sergeant "V.A. Clark!"

Virginia Clark:

> "I spotted the reference while viewing the pilot and I thought it was an inside joke. I'm sure that either my father or Whit thought of it. They both had _quite_ a sense of humor."

Jake and Gunner Ferde's "mug shots," which show them arrested by a Sergeant "V.A. Clark."

An interesting use of special effects occurred during the scene in which Superboy appears to turn coal into diamonds with the use of "super-pressure." "Si" Simonson, who only worked on this aspect of the pilot's effects, used the same approach he had on the "Superman" series, when George Reeves had to perform the same stunt.

"Si" Simonson:

> "The smoke came down the back side of John's arm out of a plastic tube that was hidden under his sleeve."

On the third day of the shoot, April 6, 1961, the scenes that involved a movie theater were filmed. The Aero Theatre was located at 1328 Montana Avenue in Santa Monica, California, and was a long-time favorite among the neighborhood children.

Virginia Clark:

> "It was a great thing for the kids to go on an expedition to the Aero Theatre. At the

SUPERBOY & SUPERPUP - THE LOST VIDEOS

John Rockwell and Bunny Henning between takes on the classroom set, ZIV Studios, 4/5/61

THE PRODUCTION OF SUPERBOY

time, we were living on 17th Street, right up from Montana Avenue, so it was always a nice little walk."

Ross Elliott (Fred Drake) in front of the Aero Theatre, 4/5/61

The Aero Theatre is still in operation as of June 1993 and continues to prosper, while several neighborhood theaters in Santa Monica have recently been torn down.

Photo by Michael J. Hayde
Author Chuck Harter in front of the Aero Theatre, 4/5/93

So popular was the Aero Theatre, in fact, that during "Superboy's" day of filming, a large crowd of children gathered to watch the Boy Of Steel come to life.

John Rockwell:

"We were on location in Santa Monica and there was a crowd of children around asking for autographs. Some of the little kids said, "How do you fly? We want to see you fly!" I didn't know what to say, so I asked Whit what to do. He said George (Reeves) used to say to the kids, "If you touch me in the right spot, I'll fly." I laughed and went over and said the same thing to the kids. Shortly thereafter, security roped off the street so we could continue."

The following week, the flying scenes for "Superboy" were shot at an unknown special effects house that was not connected with ZIV-UA. "Si" Simonson did <u>not</u> work on these scenes, but they nonetheless demonstrate a new technique used in causing Superboy to "fly." There was no special effects credit given in the end credits.

Ronnie James:

"George Reeves' series was optically matted with a traveling matte in an optical effects printer. It's all done film to film. The John Rockwell footage is obviously filmed, but then the form elements are married via video matting. It's basically the same way you'd put a weatherman in front of a map of the United States. I think Rockwell is actually being video-generated. They're shooting him with a video camera and superimposing him into, or just in front of, the filmed backgrounds of roadsides, aerial shots, and so forth. It's only married by the video. It's clever the way they did it, because it would give them more variety. You could have him doing most anything in front of them."

A unique view of Superboy flying directly into the camera was implemented. This new angle shot had <u>not</u> been used in the "Superman" series. The brief flying scene was quite effective and showed that the increased flexibility with the new video techniques could be used effectively.

John Rockwell:

> "I was hanging by wires. They made a torso cast that fit under my costume. I held my legs up myself. There was no support. The backgrounds were added later in a video production studio. While shooting, they told me, "You're flying. Now look down," etc."

The entire cast and crew seemed hopeful as the production wrapped. It had been a smooth shoot and the final cut of the pilot had been approved.

"Si" Simonson:

> "I only saw "Superboy" once. I remember thinking that Whit had done a better job in this than he had done on "Superman.""

John Rockwell:

> "They thought that after they'd seen the pilot that it was going to be sold. They'd said, "You're going to be working a lot, so you'd better get some rest.""

There was a single preview screening on the ZIV-UA lot for potential sponsors.

John Rockwell:

> "They had invited some potential sponsors, one of which was "Wheaties.""

After the screening, the representatives from Wheaties Cereals did make an offer to sponsor the series, but it was rejected.

John Rockwell:

> ""Wheaties" wanted the series, but there was a conflict with Kelloggs still having "Superman" on the air."

Apparently, Kelloggs didn't want a rival breakfast food company to sponsor a show so similar in type to the one they had sponsored for nine years. Shortly thereafter, a final print was sent to the office of D.C. Comics in New York. John was told to continue working out at the beach in preparation for the fall shooting schedule. There appeared to be great optimism that the show would be picked up during the summer. As John read a few "Superboy" comics to better understand his characterization, he noticed that the Boy Of Steel had a pet dog named Krypto. He began to train his own dog, Puff, for a part in the potential series.

John Rockwell:

> "I noticed that in the comics Superboy had a dog, so I began training him for the show. I had taught him to walk on his hind legs and to jump out of a second story window into my arms."

As the year 1961 headed into winter, there was still no word of an official acceptance or rejection of the pilot. In February of 1962, John appeared in a Los Angeles Herald Examiner newspaper regarding a court appearance. The article showcased his dog and referred to John as the "star of Superboy."

'SUPERDOG' STEALS SHOW FROM 'SUPERBOY'
TV Actor John Rockwell Lets Puff Take the Spotlight
Entering Court to Press a Car Damage Suit

THE PRODUCTION OF SUPERBOY

Attends Court
Superdog Outstars Superboy

Actor John Rockwell, 23, who plays the TV role of "Superboy," showed up in court today to press a car damage suit, but his "super dog" Puff stole the spotlight.

Puff, a shaggy white French poodle, walked on his hind legs front paws in the air, through the corridors and into Small Claims Court as attaches and bystanders stared

Rockwell said Puff can leap 25 feet through the air and knows how to open and close doors and turn on a television set.

The actor of 4606 Cresthill Rd., asked for $125 damages from Sol Weinstein charging that the latter's car banged into Rockwell's sports car last Nov. 10 at Gower and Lexington streets. Hollywood Municipal Judge Max B. Zimmerman took the case under submission after Weinsten denied his car was involved.

Puff, an interested spectator during the hearing, walked out of the courtroom the same way he came in— on his hind paws

---

As late as June of 1962, in the Vol. No. 1 issue of the magazine *Screen Thrills Illustrated*, there was a brief mention on the pending series in an article called *The Saga Of Superman*. At the end of the article, an announcement was made that in the next issue -- "for the first time you will learn...who will play the part of Superboy in a forthcoming TV series." Sadly, there was no further mention of the proposed series in the next issue. By the summer of 1962, John had received official notification that the series was not going to be produced.

John Rockwell:

> "I was told that Kelloggs didn't want it sold because of "Superman." There was a conflict with "Superman" still being on the air. I was disappointed. I thought at the time I'd be working and making some money."

In a promotional flyer for the *Flamingo Films Company*, which was distributed in early 1961, *The Adventures Of Superman* was offered for the first time in five days per week syndication. The Arbitron ratings showed that "Superman" was still very popular in several major markets. The "Superman" series had been continually on the air for nine years and the image of George Reeves as the Man Of Steel had been firmly etched into the collective consciousness of a generation of children. Perhaps there was some doubt as to whether a new actor could be accepted in the same role, even though the character would have depicted him as a youth.

Ben Chapman:

> "George Reeves was typecast as Superman. All you saw in your mind's eye was Reeves as Superman. George was so good in the part that another actor was not accepted. He also had a tremendous following from the series."

Ronnie James:

> "By 1962, the first-run syndication of quality, dramatic programming had decreased sharply. The projected "Superboy" series was probably a little too expensive for its intended market. I can't imagine that it would have been first-run on Saturday mornings. So, the only place it would have played would probably have been early evenings on Sundays. That seemed to have been the oasis of those types of programs in the early '60's. You had "Lassie" there, "National Velvet," and shows like that. I'm guessing that the price tag that was asked for it was a little too high."

John Rockwell continued to work in the acting profession after the demise of "Superboy."

John Rockwell:

> "I did some TV shows. I did one called "Dobie Gillis" with Warren Beatty and I also worked on "Ozzie and Harriet." I did quite a few movies. "The Best Of Everything," with Joan Crawford and Bob Evans, "Please Don't Eat The Daisies," with Doris Day, and a couple of things for Walt Disney. I also did a film with Ann-Margret called "Bus Riley's Back In Town." I worked in the acting profession until 1967."

In that year, an article appeared in a monster magazine called *Larry Ivie's Monsters And Heroes*, No. 2, 1967. The "Superboy" pilot was mentioned in an article, and two photographs of John Rockwell as Superboy were displayed. Unfortunately, there was not much information on the pilot. In 1974, in D.C. Comics' own publication, *The Amazing World Of D.C. Comics*, there appeared a four page article by Allan Asherman on the "Superboy" pilot. This work contained much information as well as several interesting photos of John in the title role. Further written references to the pilot appeared in such magazines as *Movie Monsters*, Vol. 1, No. 2, February 1975 in which no photos were printed, and *Fantastic Films*, Vol. 1, No. 2, June 1978, which contained a small article and two photographs that had been previously printed in *Larry Ivie's Monsters And Heroes*.

When Gary Grossman's *Superman: Serial To Cereal* book appeared in 1976, a full page reference to the pilot was printed, along with a new photograph of John Rockwell in the title role.

In the 1970's, John Rockwell spent a great deal of time with Playboy czar, Hugh Hefner. They had met almost twenty years earlier.

John Rockwell:

"I was a lifeguard when I came out from Pennsylvania, at the Beverly Hills Hotel in 1958. I saved his life when he was drowning. In 1972 in Vegas, at a backgammon tournament, I ran into him again. He invited me up to the house to play backgammon. From '72 to '78 off and on, I lived at the Playboy mansion. As a matter of fact, when I was living up at the mansion, we tried to find the "Superboy" pilot, but couldn't."

By the mid-1980's, The Adventures Of Superboy pilot had surfaced at memorabilia conventions on videotapes coupled with the "Superpup" pilot. As in the case of "Superpup," several of those people who were interviewed for this book, had not seen the "Superboy" pilot since 1961, or had never seen it. After viewing it again, the opinions were positive.

Jane Ellsworth:

"Well, I liked the young man. He was excellent. I thought he wasn't a professional yet, but I thought he would make it. It really would have been a very good show."

Patricia Ellsworth Wilson:

"I think the pilot is good. I think Rockwell was very good. Very attractive and good looking. He had a very pretty smile."

"Si" Simonson:

"I thought in watching "Superboy," that he (John Rockwell) had done an excellent job. My wife and I enjoyed it very much."

John Rockwell:

"Seeing it brought back some happy memories and it was enjoyable seeing it again. I feel the pilot could have been done better, but I still think the kids would have liked it."

Dick Rawlings:

"It was a cute show."

Virginia Clark:

"I thought it was tremendous fun to watch. It was really a kind of good slice of early American morays and kind of kitschy and fun."

In October of 1988, a new series, entitled *Superboy*, appeared on the NBC Network and went into syndication for a run of twenty-six episodes. It starred John Haymes Newton as Clark Kent/Superboy, and Stacy Haiduk as Lana Lang.

For the second season, begun in October of 1989, a change in the cast occurred, with a new actor, Gerard Christopher, taking over the part of Clark Kent/Superboy. The title was changed to *The Adventures Of Superboy*, and the series moved from NBC to general syndication. This season also ran for twenty-six episodes and was quite popular.

The series then began a third season in October of 1990, and has proven to be a quality entry into the syndicated market. For this third series, many of the stories and characters were taken directly from the D.C. Comic books, and the results were well received by the regular viewers.

The original "Adventures Of Superboy" with John Rockwell, was an interesting example of early 1960's television, and although the series never saw the light of day, it remains a respectful adaptation of the "Superman" legend.

. . .

The following list depicts those characters that were portrayed by the actors in the "Superboy" pilot, as those designations were not made in the original credits.

Clark Kent/Superboy	John Rockwell
Lana Lang	Bunny Henning
Fred Drake	Ross Elliott
Mrs. Martha Kent	Monty Margetts
Gunner Ferde	Charles Maxwell
Police Chief Parker	Robert Williams
Shifty Barnes	Richard Reeves
Miss Gibson	Yvonne White
Jake Ferde	Stacy Harris
Jimmie Drake	Jimmy Bates
Mr. Edmond	Ray Walker
Donna Givney	Trudy Ellison

THE PRODUCTION OF SUPERBOY

Original Credits...

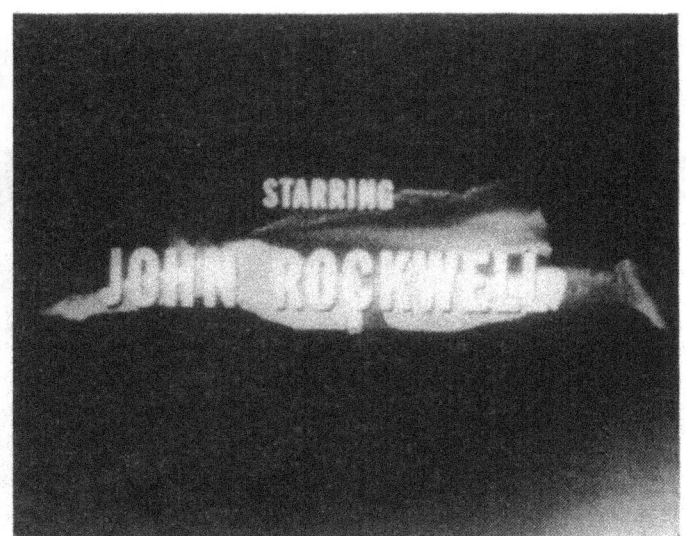

SUPERBOY & SUPERPUP - THE LOST VIDEOS

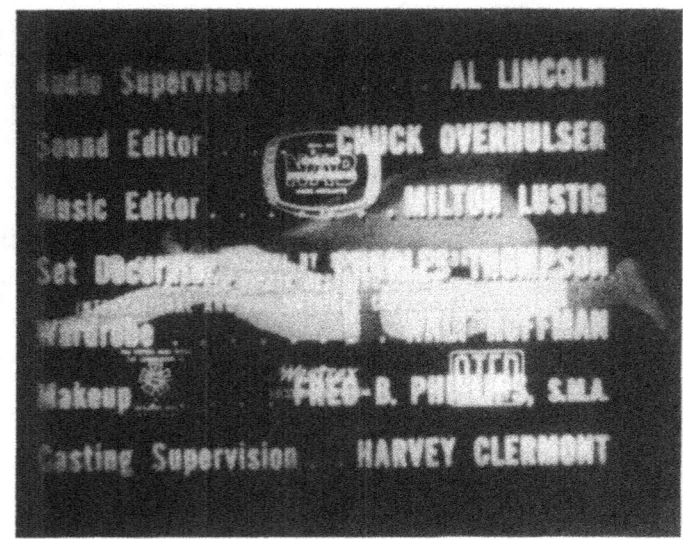

THE PRODUCTION OF SUPERBOY

Photo by Michael J. Hayde

John Rockwell at his West Hollywood apartment in a recent photo.

SUPERBOY & SUPERPUP - THE LOST VIDEOS

John Rockwell in "The Adventures Of Superboy," 1961

Chapter 6

THE SERIES THAT MIGHT HAVE BEEN

(The Twelve Unfilmed Superboy Scripts)

Along with *Rajah's Ransom*, the script of the Superboy pilot, there exist twelve additional scripts for the proposed *Adventures Of Superboy* series. They range in content from crime stories (*The Big Fence; Oil's Well; One-Man Team*) to human interest shows (*Super-Brave; Superboy's New Parents; John Doe, Superboy*) with the majority of the tales featuring science fiction themes. These could have been the most interesting and would have covered such diverse subjects as aliens from another world (*Tie Game*), time travel to ancient Greece (*Achilles Was A Heel*), a girl robot from outer space (*The Girl On The Asteroid*), a Kryptonian weapon which turns Superboy into a wraith (*The Box From Krypton*), time travel to the Old West with Mr. Mxyztplk, a creature that was featured in the D.C. Comics stories (*Superboy Out West*), and an energy absorbing machine (*Superboy Vs. Superboy*).

Some of the unfilmed scripts have similar themes to previous "Superman" TV shows such as *Tie Game*, which had an alien theme much like "Superman's" *Mr. Zero*, and *Super-Brave*, which bore some resemblance to *Test Of A Warrior*.

All of the scripts were co-written by producer Whitney Ellsworth and were copyrighted in 1961 by Superman, Inc. with the exception of *Tie Game* which carried a copyright date of 1960. Some scripts featured *Rajah's Ransom* co-writer Vernon Clark, but the bulk of the scripts credited Robert Leslie Bellem as co-author. Bellem had worked with Ellsworth on most of the 1957 Superman season's scripts such as *Divide and Conquer, The Mysterious Cube, The Perils Of Superman*, and the final episode, *All That Glitters*.

Two of the season's scripts may have had their origin in the Superboy comic books. These included the pilot *Rajah's Ransom*, which is an almost identical copy of *The Saddest Boy In Smallville*, and *One Man Team*, which is quite similar to a story called, appropriately, *One Man Team*. Both of these stories appeared in the comic book *Superboy*, #88, April, 1961. The Superboy pilot was filmed in April, 1961. Since comic books were published several months ahead of their copyright date, and it is not known in what months the Superboy scripts were written, one cannot determine which preceded the other, but the parallel plots are unmistakable.

The majority of the writing was on a par with the better "Superman" TV scripts, with several showing the potential of surpassing the later "Superman" seasons' efforts. On the whole, the entire season's scripts were quite promising, which makes the pilot's rejection even more tragic.

Regular characters on the series who appeared in more than one script, included Jonathan and Martha Kent, Lana Lang and her father, Professor Lang, Police chief Parker and, of course, Clark Kent/Superboy. Recurring sets would have depicted the Kent General store, the Kent home, Smallville High School, and the Lang house. Underground tunnels were to be located under both the Kent store and home. These tunnels would have been used to enable Superboy to come and go without detection. Superboy would have been equipped with a special radio receiver, located under the Kent home, which would only receive transmissions from Police Chief Parker and Professor Lang. A flickering lamp, located in the Kent living room, would have served as a signal that the radio was receiving a transmission. The radio and lamp were used in the *Superboy* comics, and both were featured in the *Rajah's Ransom* pilot. Most of the stories feature a great deal of exterior shooting, unlike the later "Superman" episodes, which due to increased costs of color filming, became almost totally stagebound.

Nearly all of Superboy's "super-powers" would have been used in the series, including flight, invulnerability, X-ray and telescopic vision, super-strength, super-breath and super-hearing. An interesting <u>new</u> effect would be the depiction of super-speed through the use of an animated streak of smoke. Super-speed had been utilized in the several Kellogg's Cereals commercials of the 1950's that featured George Reeves, but in those cases, a piece of board was merely whisked by the camera.

In continuing the "Superman" series tradition, most of the gangster villains were given names that could have come from the pen of Damon Runyon.

On the following pages, story board illustrations (using photos of John Rockwell along with newly drawn backgrounds) are used to offer a visual interpretation of a scene from each of the episodes. All captions are taken from the original scripts. In addition, plot synopses are given to enable readers to use their imaginations to get a clear picture of the "series that might have been."

SUPERBOY & SUPERPUP - THE LOST VIDEOS

THE BIG FENCE - {EXTERIOR - MINE - DAY - (FX)} *The tunnel entrance is completely blocked by the earthslide. But as we watch, the earth and rocks erupt outward and Superboy emerges.* - (Scene 104 - Page 39)

THE SERIES THAT MIGHT HAVE BEEN

"THE BIG FENCE"
SUPERBOY #1

Written by
Robert Leslie Bellem and Whitney Ellsworth

The episode opens with Clark Kent using his super-speed to get dressed and eat breakfast at the Kent home on a Saturday. Later, at the store, Jonathan Kent informs his adopted son that because of a new store's operation across the street, business has practically dropped off to nothing. They notice that Fleming and Larsen, the new store's owners, and their two husky helpers, Basher and Muscles, are unloading merchandise from a huge truck marked "J.B. Adams Warehouse."

Police Chief Parker enters the Kent store and is told by Jonathan that business is continuing to be very bad and that Clark suspects the new store may be selling stolen goods. Parker replies that he has investigated that possibility, but the new store seems to be legitimate. After Parker's leaving, Fleming enters the store with a small camera case in which he has hidden a tape recorder. He offers to buy out the Kent Store at twenty-five cents on the dollar. Jonathan Kent refuses and Larsen departs, leaving his camera case-recorder behind.

Professor Lang and Lana arrive and inform the Kents that they have reluctantly bought a refrigerator from the new store due to the extreme low cost. When informed of the actual price, Jonathan is astonished to find that the cost of the refrigerator is below what he has to pay at the wholesale rate.

After the Langs leave, Clark ducks into a store room located in the rear of the store, changes to Superboy, and drops down through a trapdoor into an underground tunnel which leads to the outskirts of Smallville. Superboy flies to the J.B. Adams Company, located in Metropolis, and confers with the President. He questions Adams about a new store in Smallville called the Larsen and Fleming Emporium. Adams replies that the men have paid cash at the standard wholesale rate and seem quite honest. When Superboy makes a remark about the large size of the delivery trucks, Adams produces a photograph which shows a typical Adams delivery truck which is much smaller. Adams also says that the driver who delivers to Smallville, Charlie Humboldt, is honest and respected by the firm.

Superboy flies back to the tunnel that leads to the Kent store, changes back to Clark and informs his father that Larsen, and his partner Fleming, are crooks. They buy a small truckload of goods from the Adams Warehouse, then switch to a larger truck with stolen goods from their own warehouse. Jonathan suggests they tell Chief Parker of this discovery, but Superboy vetoes the idea stating that to do so would reveal his secret identity.

Fleming soon returns to the Kent store, retrieves his camera case, then departs. When the villains play back the tape, they learn that they have been discovered. Fortunately for Clark, the tape ends just before he revealed his secret identity. Fleming then contacts Basher, who is driving toward the hidden warehouse, and instructs him not to proceed, as Superboy is onto them.

Superboy spies the truck from the air and lands in the street facing the oncoming vehicle. The truck runs over him and the two henchmen drop his apparently lifeless body into a ditch. They then drive toward the secret warehouse, convinced of Superboy's death. Back at the villain's office above their store, Fleming decides to get rid of the Kents by sealing them in an abandoned mine tunnel on the outskirts of Smallville. Superboy soon "recovers" and leaps into the air in pursuit of the truck.

Meanwhile, Superboy has spotted a smaller, legitimate warehouse truck and lands on the roof to accompany the driver, Charlie Humboldt, to the Adams Warehouse. Later, in Adam's office, Humboldt reveals that he has cooperated with the crooks because they have threatened to reveal that he is an ex-con. He wishes to make amends, and agrees to divulge the location of the hideout warehouse.

Superboy returns to Smallville and enters the Kent store as Clark. He is apprehended by Larsen and Fleming, who take him to his father, who is bound in the mine. Clark uses his X-ray vision to cause the mine's roof to collapse. The crooks panic and run for the opening where they are knocked unconscious by the cave-in. Clark shields his father from harm with his invulnerable body. He changes to Superboy and bursts through the mine's blocked entrance. (See illustration at left.)

When the crooks recover, they are tied up. Superboy leaves to alert the police. The crooks, believing that they have discovered Superboy's secret identity since Clark was the one trapped in the mine while Superboy emerged, urge Jonathan to make a deal. Superboy, however, re-enters the mine at super-speed and emerges as the shaken Clark, thus destroying the crooks' suspicions and preserving his secret identity once again.

SUPERBOY & SUPERPUP - THE LOST VIDEOS

TIE GAME - {EXT. DESERT - DAY - FULL GROUP SHOT - (FX)} *Klug and Slith remain in b.g. near the spaceship while Superboy stands in front of Leader, and persuasively addresses him.* SUPERBOY: "So you see, Mister Leader, it's foolish to start a war with Earth. Why don't you go back peaceably where you came from?" LEADER: *(draws weird gun from belt)* "You see this?" SUPERBOY: "Yes...looks like a gun." LEADER: "It's a <u>disintegrator</u> gun." *(aims)* "All right. Goodbye forever, Earthling!" *(He presses the trigger.)* {HISS - CRACKLE - ZAP!} SUPERBOY: {(FX)} *(as the disintegrator rays bounce off him)* SLITH and KLUG: *(looking off at the above with startled wonderment)* SLITH: *(awed)* "Look -- it doesn't even set fire to his clothes!" (Scenes 77, 79, 80, 81 - pages 30-31)

THE SERIES THAT MIGHT HAVE BEEN

"TIE GAME"
SUPERBOY #2

Written by
Robert Leslie Bellem and Whitney Ellsworth

It is evening in the Kent home. Lana Lang has dropped by to ask Clark to help her with some homework. Before they can begin, Jonathan Kent asks them if they might wait until he can hear the evening news on the radio. They agree, and the elder Kent tunes in the broadcast. The announcer reports that an unidentified flying object has been circling over the central desert area for three days, and has landed that morning. No sign of life has been observed, and defense authorities are meeting in Washington to determine what course of action to take. Soon, tanks, artillery, and several divisions of the infantry have been ordered to the area. Clark, realizing his sudden need to change identities, abruptly asks Lana to leave the house, under the pretext of a suddenly remembered appointment.

Clark changes to Superboy, and flies to the Pentagon in Washington, D.C., to confer with military leaders. There, the Boy Of Steel convinces the top brass that if the ship were from another planet and they have the ability to travel to Earth, then they might have superior weapons, that could destroy all life on Earth. He asks that they wait one hour before any aggressive action is taken, so that he may have a chance of repelling the invaders with no loss of human life. The military leaders order all personnel and equipment to an immediate halt, and grant Superboy one hour before they will launch a full-scale attack.

When Superboy arrives at the saucer's location, a door in the ship opens to reveal an alien who is called "The Leader." Described in the script as "a massive bruiser in weird garb, with a face to match," he is joined by two similar looking underlings, Slith and Klug. Despite Superboy's friendly approach, the aliens admit they are, in fact, from another planet, and are on a hostile mission. Superboy tells them that he is a typical Earthling and asks them to leave. The Leader orders Slith and Klug to "best" Superboy and demonstrate their superiority.

After attempting several tests of Superboy's strength such as hand gripping, punching and wrestling, the aliens begin to suspect that if indeed Superboy is a typical Earthling, then it might not be so easy to conquer the planet. They even strike Superboy with a super-hard truncheon, which breaks on contact. These tests use up the hour that the military heads have granted Superboy and the order is given to send a full-scale attack upon the alien craft.

In desperation, the aliens shoot at Superboy with a disintegrator gun which has no ill effect upon the Boy Of Steel. (See illustration at left.) Superboy melts the gun with his X-ray vision. The aliens then boast that their ship is made of a super metal alloy, which nothing can penetrate. Superboy attempts to break through the ship's surface and bounces off the impregnable hull. He then proposes that since the aliens could not harm him and he couldn't penetrate their ship's surface, that they call the situation a tie game.

Both sides agree that since there has been no loss of honor on either side, a stalemate has been achieved. The aliens, also believing Superboy to be a typical Earthling, agree to leave immediately and abandon their invasion plans. Before leaving, they give Superboy a sample of the indestructible metal used on their ship's surface as a souvenir. They then depart, moments before the military arrives on the scene.

Back at the Pentagon, Superboy astounds the military leaders by casually tearing the alien's indestructible metal in half. He could have broken through the ship's surface, but chose not to so, since they wouldn't be able to leave with a broken ship. The aliens were given a "tie-game" situation, which afforded them an honorable excuse to leave Earth with a degree of dignity.

SUPERBOY & SUPERPUP - THE LOST VIDEOS

ACHILLES WAS A HEEL - {GROUP SHOT (FX)} *Now Trigoon, gloweringly, slowly draws his sword and advances on Superboy. Suddenly, he lunges, the point of the sword directly at Superboy's heart. But the sword curls up like a piece of paper.* - (Scene 67 - page 67)

THE SERIES THAT MIGHT HAVE BEEN

"ACHILLES WAS A HEEL"
SUPERBOY #3

Written by
Robert Leslie Bellem and Whitney Ellsworth

The story opens at the Kent General Store. Jonathan and Clark are both present when Professor Periwinkle enters. He is described in the script as "a vague looking middle-aged man, perpetually wool-gathering." He asks Clark to help him find the Kent Store and is reminded that he *is* in it. The Professor has brought four dozen eggs to trade for groceries. He mysteriously says that the eggs were "laid tomorrow." Clark and Jonathan wonder about this announcement, but agree to the trade. The kindly Jonathan even gives the Professor $1.25 in change whereby Periwinkle exits the store but leaves the bag of groceries behind.

Lana Lang soon drops by the store on her bicycle, complaining of heavy static on the family radio. She is told that all of the Kent's customers have been complaining of the same problem and that the source of it has not been found. Lana notices the Professor's bag of groceries and agrees to deliver them to his shack.

When she arrives, Professor Periwinkle explains that he has invented a time machine that he has been using to retrieve eggs that his hens have been laying twenty four hours in the future. Hence, the eggs are "laid tomorrow." Her curiosity aroused, Lana soon enters the machine and disappears into the past. Meanwhile, Clark changes to Superboy and using his super-hearing discovers that the source of the radios' static has been coming from the Professor's shack.

Upon arriving, Superboy soon learns of Lana's disappearance and is told by the absent-minded Professor that there are four periods in past history that Lana may have gone into. Professor Perriwinkle doesn't know which era, due to the fact that he twisted the dials, and can't remember their original settings. After reaffirming the Professor's forgetfulness, and wishing to protect his secret identity from Lana, Superboy changes to Clark Kent and enters the time machine with the Professor. Once they arrive in Ancient Rome and Egypt, Clark uses his X-ray vision, and does not find Lana among the populations. They next arrive in Ancient Greece, where Lana is discovered on the outskirts of Athens. Both are surprised to see her in a Grecian robe. She explains that her clothes are being washed and that she has been befriended by the legendary hero, Hercules, and his sister Herculina.

Hercules, the number one hero of Greece, who has never lost a fight, has taken to the hills to recover from a back injury so that he may continue to defend his position. Achilles, the number two hero, and his henchman Trigoon, appear and capture Lana and Herculina. Achilles intends to force the injured Hercules into a fight that he cannot win. The villain threatens to sell the girls as slaves to a rich King after he defeats Hercules. Clark suggests that *he* fight Achilles as Hercules' proxy as that practice *is* allowed by the code of Ancient Greece.

Young Kent departs and soon reappears as Superboy and prepares to do battle with Achilles. Achilles commands Trigoon to be *his* proxy, and after failing to harm the Boy Of Steel with punches and kicks, attempts to stab him with a sword. But the sword curls up like paper and has no effect on Superboy. (See illustration at left.) Achilles then lunges at Superboy and injures *his* back after colliding with the teen titan's invulnerable body. Achilles and Trigoon vow to release the captured girls before their return to Athens. Hercules' position as the number one Hero has remained intact. Superboy changes back to Clark before the girls' return, with Hercules' and the Professor's vows of silence as to his dual identity, and informs them of Hercules' "victory" over Achilles.

The Professor, Clark and Lana return to Smallville, whereupon Lana realizes that she is still wearing the Grecian robe and has left her modern clothes behind. She attempts to re-enter the time machine, but is held back by Clark as the Professor smashes the device while declaring, "if any more eggs ever come out of *this* machine, they'll be scrambled.

SUPERBOY & SUPERPUP - THE LOST VIDEOS

OIL'S WELL - {EXT. HIGHWAY - DAY} - *(As the hood pops up, Superboy reaches swiftly in, comes up with the now-reeking bomb. He draws back his arm and hurls the bomb {OVER CAMERA}.* - (Scene 90 - page 32)

"OIL'S WELL"
SUPERBOY #4

Written by
Robert Leslie Bellem and Whitney Ellsworth

The opening finds Clark Kent and Lana Lang driving to some property owned by her father, Professor Lang, on the outskirts of Smallville. They intend to have a picnic. As they approach the edge of the property, they notice a "Closed - Keep Out" sign. Clark suggests they turn back, but Lana insists on going ahead. They prepare to move the sign, when Ox McGonigle, described in the script as "a huge rugged man...capable of anything," stops them. Lana protests that her father owns the land, but Ox persuades them to return to Smallville.

Back at the Lang house, as Lana complains of the rejection, the Professor reveals that George Wellington and Victor Vernon, two overdressed businessmen, are his new partners. Both men claim to be geologists, and they have reason to believe that there may be oil under Lang's "worthless" property. At present, they are drilling a shallow well for testing. Clark mentions several geological terms, and drawing blank stares from the two men, exits, his suspicions aroused.

Later, after changing to Superboy, he flies to the location of the oil rig, and observes Ox, Wellington and Vernon, apparently at work. His curiosity satisfied, he returns to Smallville.

Later, Professor Lang explains to the "geologists" that Jonathan Kent has agreed to act as secretary-treasurer if they get to the point of selling stock to finance the drilling of a deep well. The next day at the oil rig, Wellington, Vernon and Ox bury ten drums of crude oil in the earth, and plan to create the illusion of an oil strike by use of an underground pump. When Wellington worries that Superboy might discover their ruse through the use of his X-ray vision, the others suggest painting the rig platform with lead paint so that Superboy cannot see through it and expose them.

Later that day in the Kent store, Jonathan Kent is handing out stock certificates to what seems like the entire population of Smallville, all of whom are eager to invest their money. Clark, suspicious, leaves, and after changing to Superboy, flies to the oil rig for further investigation.

The villains persuade Jonathan Kent that it would be good for business to take the peoples' money and put it in the Amalgamated Trust Company of Metropolis for safekeeping. Kent puts the money in a briefcase, and while his attention is diverted, the crooks switch briefcases so that the real money is replaced by blank paper.

Meanwhile, at the oil rig, Superboy finds an empty lead paint can. Suspicious, he rips up a plank of the platform and discovers the ten gallon drums and pump. Lana, Professor Lang and Jonathan Kent set off in the Lang car for Metropolis with the switched briefcase in the back seat. They are unaware that the villains have rigged a napalm bomb to go off when their drained radiator overheats; not only to destroy them, but to give the appearance of the money's having been destroyed as well. As they proceed into the country, the car's engine begins to smoke.

Suddenly, Superboy appears, pops open the hood, and hurls the bomb into the air where it explodes harmlessly. (See illustration at left.) He informs the dazed passengers that Vernon and Wellington are crooks and that he has a plan to make them return of their own free will with the money. He promises to send someone with water for their car and departs for the Gordon Oil Company.

Meeting with the company president, Superboy asks for enough crude oil to make the Lang property appear drenched. The oil president agrees to help and also offers the use of his radio station. The villains, after driving two thousand miles away from Smallville, tune in a news broadcast and are shocked to hear that the Lang property has yielded a gusher and that the people of Smallville, the stockholders, are rich. The radio also reveals the tragic deaths of Professor Lang, Lana, and Jonathan Kent in a car explosion.

Falling for the bait, the crooks immediately return to Smallville where they attempt to buy back the stock from Mr. Gordon, at one hundred percent interest to the stockholders. After they do so, Jonathan Kent appears and confronts them with their guilt. Superboy soon arrives and overpowers the con men. All monies are returned, and the people of Smallville decide to donate their profits to build a new hospital which is appropriately called the Wellington-Vernon-McGonigle Memorial Hospital.

SUPERBOY & SUPERPUP - THE LOST VIDEOS

THE GIRL ON THE ASTEROID - {INT. CAVE - DAY} - QUADRA: *"You see, I have no...heart. No...soul."* (beat) *"I'm only a robot."* SUPERBOY: (breathily disbelieving) *"Oh, no...no, Quadra..."* - (Scenes 53-55 - pages 31-32)

THE SERIES THAT MIGHT HAVE BEEN

"THE GIRL ON THE ASTEROID"
SUPERBOY #5

Written by
Robert Leslie Bellem and Whitney Ellsworth

It is evening at the Kent home. Lana Lang has dropped by to borrow some sugar as the heavy rains that Smallville has been experiencing has prevented her from going out to the store. The Kents tune into a radio broadcast and discover that many natural disasters such as tornadoes, heavy rainstorms, and hurricanes are plaguing the entire planet.

After Lana leaves, Clark changes to Superboy and flies to Metropolis to confer with Professor Billings, Director of the International Scientific Council, in the hope of finding an explanation for the recent disasters. Superboy is told that the Council has discovered the source of the disaster and has not informed the news media to avoid a mass panic.

It seems that the unusual weather conditions are being caused by an asteroid which was hurled into space when a dark star exploded. The asteroid is also surrounded by a ring of radioactive particles. The eccentric orbit of the asteroid is causing a change in the terrestrial balance and is not only producing freak weather conditions, but is set on a collision course for Earth. The Earth is doomed. When asked by Superboy whether there has been any attempts to destroy the asteroid, Professor Billings replies that several nuclear-armed satellite projectiles have been secretly launched with no ill effect, since the asteroid's ring of particles deflected them from their course.

However, all hope is not lost as there is a super-bomb that could destroy the asteroid, but there appears to be no way to get it past the deflection. The Boy Of Steel volunteers to fly the small super-bomb into space, and carrying it under his arm, leaps into the sky. As Superboy approaches the asteroid's dust cloud, he tumbles and lands on the asteroid, knocking himself unconscious.

Upon regaining his senses, he discovers that Quadra, described in the script as "a cute young girl in an outlandish, but attractive costume" is attending to a deep gash across his forehead. She claims to have telepathic powers and knows of Superboy's secret identity of Clark Kent. Quadra explains that the asteroid is all that remains of her home planet Excelsis and that she is the sole survivor of her doomed world. Superboy is in a very weakened state and after attempting to fly, falls to the asteroid's surface, once again becoming unconscious.

Meanwhile on Earth, Professor Billings announces on the radio that the planet is being approached on a collision course by the asteroid and that Superboy has flown into space in an attempt to deflect it. However, the scientist has discovered that the dust ring around the asteroid contains Kryptonite and that Superboy may be unable to help the Earth. While listening to this broadcast at the Lang home, the Kents hide their fears for their adopted son's safety from Lana, who has been told that Clark is in Metropolis. She is upset that he hasn't been in touch.

On the asteroid, Quadra informs the Boy Of Steel that his weakened condition is a result of the Kryptonite rays. Superboy tells her that he would gladly sacrifice himself and set off the super-bomb, but doesn't wish to harm her. The mysterious girl displays several examples of super-strength and when asked by Superboy whether she can fly, replies that was the one thing "they" didn't think of. When asked by Superboy if there is any lead on the planet for protection from the Kryptonite's rays, Quadra takes him to a cave and shows him a sheet of lead used for "repairs." The strange girl then fashions the lead into a protective helmet for the Boy Of Steel.

Superboy promises to take Quadra to Earth with him and is stunned when she informs him that she is a robot and would have no place in his world. (See illustration at left.) He tells her that she is a real person and he will take her with him and that they will keep each other's secrets.

Superboy dons the completed helmet, and regains his strength. Quadra suggest a short test flight to insure that his powers have fully returned. He agrees and while flying, Quadra, a tear in her eye and firm in her belief that she would have no place in Superboy's world, sets off the super-bomb, thus destroying herself and the asteroid.

After Superboy returns sadly to Earth, Professor Billings announces in a radio broadcast that the Boy Of Steel has saved the planet, but has said that he was not alone in being responsible for the feat.

Later, at the Kent home, Lana complains to Clark that her didn't contact her while in Metropolis. He apologizes and tells her that he learned something while away. One must never forget a friend, because you don't always have them forever.

SUPERBOY & SUPERPUP - THE LOST VIDEOS

SUPER-BRAVE - {EXT. ENCAMPMENT - DAY} - *SUPERBOY: "Now you really are their chief."* (turns) *"And the time has come for me to return to my own people. I will send police to pick up the paleface bad men...and as a remembrance, I would like to have this Superboy costume."* - (Scene 102 - page 40)

THE SERIES THAT MIGHT HAVE BEEN

"SUPER-BRAVE"
SUPERBOY #6

Written by
Robert Leslie Bellem and Whitney Ellsworth

The story opens with a forest fire which is rapidly approaching a boys' summer camp. A group of Indian youths in native costume, are seated in a circle at the camp. They are awaiting the return of Tall Arrow, the camp's chief-counselor, who finally appears, with a broken leg. He tells the boys that the fire is creeping toward them from all sides and that there is no hope of escape. They all agree to stoically await their fate, and to die with dignity.

Meanwhile, in a cheap motel, two crooks, Lifter Mobray and Knuckles Grogan, are regarding the news of the forest fire with disgust. They had planned to steal the Indian boys' relics, located in a shack, to sell to a wealthy collector. The fire will prevent them from reaching Beaver Valley and heisting the valuable relics.

The Kent family hears of the blaze during a radio broadcast, which prompts Clark to change into Superboy and fly to the boys' rescue. The Boy Of Steel soon lands at the indian boys' camp and uses his super-breath to blow out the forest fire. He examines Tall Arrow's leg and confirms that it _is_ indeed broken. Tall Arrow permits his wound to be attended, then goes to the relic shack to heal according to the tribe's ancient custom.

Knuckles and Lifter hear of the suffocated fire over the radio, and resume their plan to steal the relics.

In the relic shack, Tall Arrow explains to Superboy that although the boys live the white man's ways and attend his schools, during the summer they go to the camp to preserve their ancient customs and traditions. They bring the relics as reminders of the tribe's past greatness. Tall Arrow tells Superboy that an election must be held to appoint a new chief-counselor to assume leadership while his wound heals.

The dishonest Grey Elk rigs the election so that he, and not the more popular Eagle Feather, wins. Superboy witnesses Grey Elk's trickery, but chooses not to interfere for the time being. He bids the tribe farewell and returns to Smallville. With Superboy gone, Grey Elk begins abusing his new position.

Back in Smallville, Clark discusses the tribe's situation with his parents who persuade him to return and keep an eye on Grey Elk. He agrees, and planning to adopt a disguise, acquires some theatrical makeup from his dad's store. At the camp, Grey Elk demands to be served his meals, _and_ insists that the boys make him a Superboy costume. When this is done, he takes the new name of Super Brave.

Superboy arrives at the camp and, in make-up, calls himself Red Pony. Super Brave challenges the disguised Boy Of Steel to compete in some games of skill and tests of strength. Red Pony quickly defeats Super Brave at wrestling and arrow shooting to the delight of the rest of the boys.

Meanwhile, Knuckles and Lifter are preparing to parachute out of a plane as it flies over the boys' camp. After they land, Superboy tells Grey Elk that two armed men are approaching the relic shack. Tall Arrow, inside the shack, cries out in alarm, but is soon bound and gagged by Lifter. In his makeshift Superboy costume, Grey Elk bursts into the relic shack. Knuckles panics at the sight of the Superboy costume, throws away his gun, and attempts to flee. He impacts against the still disguised Superboy, and is knocked unconscious. Lifter, frightened by the advancing Super Brave, throws down his gun and surrenders. Superboy and Grey Elk then tie up the villains and free Tall Arrow.

Later, Grey Elk throws the makeshift Superboy costume on the ground and announces the end of Super Brave. He apologizes to the boys and says that the crooks only surrendered because they were afraid of the Superboy costume. Superboy, who has removed his makeup, replies that Grey Elk showed great bravery in facing the armed robbers. Grey Elk admits to "fixing" the election and is told by Tall Arrow that he has shown great courage by admitting his mistakes.

Superboy suggests they hold a new election and watches with happiness as Grey Elk is voted the new Chief-counselor. As he prepares to leave, Superboy promises to send the police to pick up the crooks and asks for the makeshift Superboy costume as a souvenir. (See illustration at left.)

SUPERBOY & SUPERPUP - THE LOST VIDEOS

ONE MAN TEAM - {EXT. AT STADIUM - DAY} - *PROF. LANG:* (continuing) *"Now we're going to see an 'explosive kick.'"* (Superboy takes a short run and kicks the ball.) - (Scene 91 - page 30)

THE SERIES THAT MIGHT HAVE BEEN

"ONE-MAN TEAM"
SUPERBOY #7

Written by
Vernon E. Clark and Whitney Ellsworth

The story opens with Lana Lang arriving at the Kent General Store, only to complain that Smallville High's football team is in bad shape, with no hope of a winning season. She asks Clark to join, but he declines, claiming bad eyesight.

Clark, accompanied by Lana, takes the store's receipts to the Smallville Bank. While they are there, two petty crooks, Fred Serf and Joe France, rob the bank at gunpoint. After the crooks leave, Clark runs to the Kent Store and informs his father of the robbery, He changes to Superboy and flies after the departing crooks.

He soon catches up to them and pulls their car to a stop. Serf and France exit the car, and claiming not to believe the story that Superboy is invulnerable, open fire on him. The bullets bounce off the Boy Of Steel's chest and he seizes their pistols and crushes them in his hands. He tells the crooks to drive back to Smallville, return the money and turn themselves over to the police. They agree to do so as Superboy flies back to the Kent home.

Later, in the Lang house, Professor Lang and Lana are listening to the news report of the robber's capture, when Bill Reynolds, head of the athletic committee, calls. He has heard that Lang can contact Superboy and wishes that the Professor would ask the Boy Of Steel to enroll at Smallville High School so that he could play sports on their teams. Lang agrees to this, but tells Lana that it wouldn't be fair for Superboy to play on any sports teams.

He calls the Boy Of Steel on a special radio and requests his presence. Superboy arrives, and when asked to enroll declines, but suggests that he might put on an athletic exhibition at the huge Metropolis Stadium to raise money for Smallville High.

Meanwhile, in a cheap hotel, Jack Wales and Jack Buton, two petty crooks, are dressed as hot dog vendors with a third criminal, Muscles Martin, present. They have planned to steal the stadium receipts in their vendor disguises, while Superboy is performing his athletic stunts.

The day of the exhibition, Clark elects to stay behind and watch the Kent store while the Langs and Kents travel to Metropolis. After they leave, Clark puts a CLOSED sign in the store window, changes to Superboy, and flies to Metropolis.

At the stadium, which is filled to capacity, Professor Lang announces over the P.A. system that Superboy will soon be arriving. When Superboy lands, he makes a speech to the effect that the _best_ team is one that puts one hundred percent effort on every play and that the _playing_, not the scoring, is the most important thing. The crowd cheers his speech with much enthusiasm.

For his first stunt, Superboy takes a baseball, and from a distance of sixty feet, hits a two inch circle on a wooden plank. He then takes a baseball bat and bunts a ball which disappears into the ground. The crowd reacts to the stunts with applause and awe.

Meanwhile, the three crooks, all dressed as hot dog vendors, prepare to hold up the box office.

For his next stunt, Superboy announces that he will perform an "explosive kick" on a football. He takes a short run and kicks the ball. (See illustration at left.) The ball explodes on contact as the crowd cheers. He then takes a lighter approach and kicks another football clear out of the stadium.

Just then, a policeman informs Superboy that the box office has been robbed by three men dressed as vendors. Superboy leaps to the top parapet of the stadium and locates the fleeing villains' car with his telescopic vision. He returns to the playing field, and taking a policeman's tear gas grenade, throws it out of the stadium at the crooks' car. The grenade crashes through the rear window and forces the criminals to bring their car to a halt.

Back at the playing field, Superboy lightly kicks three footballs, which soar out of the stadium and knock the three teary-eyed villains out cold. He then gives the car's location to the policeman, who calls the Highway Patrol to go an pick them up. Superboy then departs.

The exhibition a huge success, the Langs and Kents return to Smallville where they discover a sleeping Clark at the Kent home.

THE BOX FROM KRYPTON - {EXT. SECLUDED AREA - DAY} - *(CAMERA PANS UP CLOSE on a lizard resting atop the boulder.) CLOSE ON LIZARD (it moves out of scene, and for all <u>we</u> know it is jumping toward the little box.) The lizard falls on the black button. Instantly, the weapon's orifice emits sparks and rays with appropriate SOUND. ON SUPERBOY {(FX)} Suddenly he glows, and has a visible aura. He reacts.* - (Scenes 43-47 - pages 18-19)

THE SERIES THAT MIGHT HAVE BEEN

"THE BOX FROM KRYPTON"
SUPERBOY #8

Written by
Robert Leslie Bellem and Whitney Ellsworth

The story begins at the Kent General Store as Lana Lang drops by to see Clark's new electric typewriter. She is impressed by it's efficiency, and wonders if a person could just think the keys into moving. Clark replies that one's brainwaves would have to be super-strong to do so. Jonathan Kent then asks Clark to deliver a grocery order to a distant area of town. He agrees to do so, and tells Lana to practice on the typewriter while he makes up the order.

Police Chief Parker soon enters the store and asks the elder Kent about two suspicious-looking men who have been seen around town. They both notice the two men, Marty Clee and Spinner Bristol, in the street outside the store, apparently innocent of any wrongdoing. Parker asks Kent to keep his eyes open, and soon departs.

Clark shortly thereafter tells Lana to accompany him on his delivery, and says that he will take her home when finished. She leaves with him, neglecting to turn off the typewriter.

Later, at the Lang home, Professor Lang is puzzled over a mysterious sealed box sent to him from a friend in the Gobi Desert. Apparently, the box was found buried underground in the nose cone of a space rocket. Upon touching the box, Lang and Lana feel a tingling, but Clark does not. However, he does notice that the box contains Kryptonian writing on the sides. Clark makes an excuse to leave and soon Professor Lang is calling Superboy on his special radio.

Within a short time, the Boy Of Steel arrives and confirms that the box is from Krypton and that his X-ray vision is useless since the box is lined with lead.

For safety's sake, he flies the box to a deserted area outside of Smallville and opens the box with his super-strength. Inside, he finds a scroll, written in the Kryptonian language, warning that the contents are advanced weapons which have been deemed too dangerous to keep on Krypton and have been discarded by a rocket that was sent into space.

Superboy finds two ray guns inside, one of which destroys plant life, and the other which evaporates a boulder. He then finds a box weapon and is informed by the scroll that this is a device used to punish criminals by sending them into Dimension-X. Under no circumstances should the box's black button be touched.

Superboy sets the device on a rock, when suddenly, a lizard falls on the black button, causing the weapon to emit sparks and rays which hit the Boy Of Steel. (See illustration at left.) Superboy is transformed into a transparent wraith.

Attempts to touch solid objects fail, and he finally returns to the Kent store. Jonathan Kent, oblivious to Superboy's anguished cries and unable to see him, is then visited by Clee and Bristol. To avoid suspicion, they make a substantial donation to the hospital charity drive, of which Kent is treasurer, and leave.

Superboy, who had overheard the crooks discussing an upcoming armored car robbery, tries to warn his father, but doesn't succeed as he still can't be heard or seen.

Back at the Kent home, Superboy continues his attempts to contact his parents with no success.

Still later, the two crooks don gas masks and rob an armored car after they have rendered the guards unconscious with tear gas. Superboy tries to stop them, but the stolen armored car passes right through the Boy of steel. The crooks travel to their hideout, where they begin to transfer the stolen money to their own car.

Superboy returns to the Kent store, where he sees that the electric typewriter is still on. By intense concentration, he manages to spell out a message to his father, telling him of his predicament, as well as the box weapon's location. The Kents, Professor Lang and Lana travel to the weapon and, after aiming it according to the invisible Superboy's instructions, press the restorative white button.

As the sparks and rays hit him, Superboy returns to normal. He immediately crushes the weapons and box to dust, then flies off in the direction of the crooks' hideout. Arriving there, Superboy quickly overcomes the two criminals and orders them to remain there while he contacts Chief Parker to pick them up.

SUPERBOY & SUPERPUP - THE LOST VIDEOS

SUPERBOY'S NEW PARENTS - {INT. CARSON HOUSE} - *(Carson puts the cigar in his mouth and produces a lighter. But before he can light it:* SUPERBOY: *(continuing)* "Wait a second, Dad. I'll light that for you. Let me show you -- my X-ray vision's good for a lot of things." {CLOSEUP - SUPERBOY'S EYES} *They narrow, and we HEAR an electrical crackling.* {CLOSE SHOT - CARSON - (FX)} *With the cigar in his mouth. We HEAR the electrical crackling, and sparks (animation) hit the cigar. Then it bursts into flame.* - (Scenes 95-97 - page 32)

<u>THE SERIES THAT MIGHT HAVE BEEN</u>

"SUPERBOY'S NEW PARENTS"
SUPERBOY #9

Written by
Paul Harber and Whitney Ellsworth

The story opens at the modest farmhouse of Fred Carson, a small time confidence man. He is typing a letter, when his wife, Kate, arrives with several packages. Carson inquires as to whether she has picked up the chunks of rock, balloons and cloth that he requested. She replies that she has. Kate then tells him that she is tired of his schemes and wishes they could go straight. He counters that they recently made seven thousand dollars and, even though they can't spend any of it for awhile until the heat dies down, some of his schemes <u>do</u> work.

Carson shows her a newspaper headline that reads SUPERBOY TO TESTIFY AGAINST BANK ROBBERS and says that the Boy Of Steel will be appearing in court the very next day. The following afternoon in Smallville Court, Judge Davidson sentences several crooks for their participation in an armed bank robbery. He is commending Superboy for his part in apprehending the criminals, when handed a special delivery letter from a courier. Present in the courtroom are the Kents, Professor Lang, Lana and others in the spectator's gallery. The letter, from Carson, states that since Superboy is a resident of Smallville and a minor, he should be given the benefit of a supervised background like other children.

When asked by the Judge if he has any parents, Superboy, not wishing to reveal his secret identity, replies that he has no answer. Judge Davidson says that the town's laws apply to everyone and that Superboy will be remanded to the State Home for Boys until he becomes of age. Fred Carson offers to adopt Superboy and says that he and his wife will give him a good home.

When asked by the Judge as to his choice, the State Home or the Carsons, Superboy replies that he will go to the Carsons. The Judge says that the adoption papers will soon be drawn up and that Superboy must go with the couple.

Superboy tells his new parents that he will join them the following day, as he has some things to do. He then flies to the Kent home and changes to Clark. When he returns to his <u>real</u> foster parents, young Kent explains that he couldn't expose their secret in the courtroom, or criminals could get at him through them. Clark tells them not to worry, that he will return soon.

The next day, as Superboy approaches the Carson house from the air, he notices that a lot of changes have been made. There is a large banner reading "SUPERBOY-IN-PERSON -- ADMISSION ONE DOLLAR" stretched across the front yard. There are many cars parked in front, and several sight-seers are milling around. Carson, by microphone, tells the crowd that several souvenirs are for sale, such as Superboy helium balloons, imitation Kryptonite rocks, Superboy vitamin tonic and authentic Superboy costumes. The Boy Of Steel lands and is told by Carson that the people <u>want</u> to see him and he is only charging fees to cover expenses.

Professor Lang and Lana arrive and are shocked by the carnival atmosphere. When Lang tells Superboy he is being used, Superboy replies that he has a plan which will begin the next day.

In the morning, Carson is happily counting the first day's receipts, when Superboy appears and devours a huge breakfast in seconds and says he is still hungry. After he eats a whole cake in seconds, and asks for more. The Carsons begin to worry that he might eat them out of house and home. When Carson puts a cigar in his mouth, Superboy attempts to light it with his X-ray vision, but it bursts into flame, along with an end table. (See illustration at left.) Superboy quickly blows out the fires and says he <u>must</u> learn to control his X-ray vision. He then breaks an overstuffed chair by sitting in it, and creates a jet-like roar by flying over the Caron's home.

For the next three evenings he flies over the house all night, keeping his new foster parents awake. They soon agree to give up their newly adopted son.

The next day in court, Judge Davidson grants their request. With Professor Lang's help, Superboy displays superior mental and physical skills, and is judged to be a man in the eyes of the court. Carson offers to return the seven thousand dollars and go straight, to which Judge Davidson agrees, and Superboy is told that he is free to go as he pleases.

SUPERBOY OUT WEST - {INT. CAFE - DAY} *(The place is a shambles)* {ANGLE ON MA POTTS} *(leaning on the counter and weeping as if her heart would break)* SUPERBOY: *(He reacts to the above and, looking concerned, moves toward Ma Potts, putting an arm on her shoulder)* "There, there now." - (Scenes 33-37 - pages 23-24)

THE SERIES THAT MIGHT HAVE BEEN

"SUPERBOY OUT WEST"
SUPERBOY #10

Written by
Robert Leslie Bellem and Whitney Ellsworth

The story opens in the Kent living room. Professor Lang and Lana are leaving after having dinner. Jonathan Kent laments that he didn't have time to tell them about his great grandfather, who was hanged for cattle rustling, but promises to tell the story the next time they all meet.

That night, while in bed asleep, Clark is awakened by Mr. Mxyztplk, described in the script as a "very little midget-sized individual in an outlandish costume, including a bowler hat." He tells Clark that he is from the ninth dimension, and that he knows Superboy and Clark Kent are one and the same. Mr. Mxyztplk offers to take Clark back in time to any period in history he chooses.

Clark elects to return to the town of Scorpion Wells in the year 1868 and dons some western clothing leftover from a school play. He takes the imp's hand and they are soon walking on a western street. The young Kent sees a storefront sign that reads MEALS - 10¢ -- WATER - 50¢ PER GLASS, and asks the strange being why the water is so high-priced. Mr. Mxyztplk replies that an evil boss has blown up the local river, sent the water underground, and plans to buy out the local ranchers' herds.

Suddenly, gunshots fill the air, which causes the frightened creature to disappear. Rattlesnake Gallagher, a local tough, is running with a cask of water. He is pursued by Ma Potts, an elderly lady, when he runs right into Clark and is knocked unconscious. Ma Potts thanks Clark and tells him she runs the local cafe.

Sheriff Barker appears and arrests the revived Gallagher. Clark later enters the Last Chance Water Store and is surprised to see John Kent, a middle-aged westerner, Banker Jethro and their two henchmen, Blackie and Quint, seated at a nearby table.

As Clark buys a drink of water, Leila Logan, a young girl, enters and solicits contributions for a charity to buy water for the town's poor. John Kent tells her to leave, and when Clark interferes, he sends Blackie over to punch him. The henchman's fist is nearly broken from the impact and a full-scale brawl is only averted by the timely arrival of Barker.

The Sheriff informs them that Rattlesnake Gallagher is behind bars for attempting to rob Ma Potts and that Clark is responsible for his capture. Upon hearing this news, the villains depart. The bartender gives Leila and Clark drinks of water on the house and remarks that John Kent is probably figuring a way to get even with Ma Potts.

Clark goes to an alley, changes to Superboy, and heads for Ma Potts' cafe. He finds John Kent, Blackie and Quint smashing up the place and warns them to stop. They leave immediately, and Superboy comforts Ma Potts, who is leaning on the counter and weeping. (See illustration at left.)

As she goes into the unharmed kitchen, Superboy restores her cafe to pristine condition. She thanks him and he leaves, enters an alley, and changes back to Clark Kent. He borrows the bartender's horse and leaves town in pursuit of the desperadoes.

When out of town, he changes to Superboy and locates the badmen's shack with his X-ray vision, lands outside, and listens in on the villains' conversation. Inside, Banker Jethro tells his hired guns that the time has come to buy up the cattle, take them to the underground water, dynamite the stream and provide water for their new herds. John Kent agrees and Superboy, saddened to hear of his great-grandfather's villainy, flies away. He lands behind a boulder and emerges as Clark Kent, when he sees Mr. Mxyztplk reappear. Clark tells the imp that he must report Kent to the Sheriff even if it means incriminating an ancestor.

The strange being hears an approaching horse and vanishes. It is Sheriff Barker and Clark promises to take him to the badmen's shack.

Meanwhile, at the shack, John Kent prepares to leave and drops his wallet by mistake. Blackie looks inside, draws his gun and shows the wallet to Jethro, who orders Kent hung from the nearest tree. Just before they can hang him, Clark and the Sheriff arrive.

Clark uses his X-ray vision to burn a hole in the tree bark, which falls and knocks the villains out. John Kent explains that he is a detective for the Cattlemen's Association and was working undercover when the badmen discovered his badge in his wallet.

Clark leaves them to tie up the villains, changes to Superboy, and burrows into the ground, thus freeing the underground water. Mr. Mxyztplk soon appears and returns Superboy to the present.

The next day, Jonathan Kent tells Lana that his great-grandfather was really a detective and wasn't lynched, but was saved by a miracle.

SUPERBOY & SUPERPUP - THE LOST VIDEOS

JOHN DOE, SUPERBOY - {EXT. COUNTRY ROAD - DAY (FX)} - *(Superboy lands on the ground and bounces. For a moment he lies stunned.)* {CLOSER SHOT - SUPERBOY} *(He struggles unsteadily to his feet, his expression dazed.)* - (Scenes 5-6, page 2)

THE SERIES THAT MIGHT HAVE BEEN

"JOHN DOE, SUPERBOY"
SUPERBOY #11

Written by
Robert Leslie Bellem and Whitney Ellsworth

Inside the Kent home, Jonathan and Martha are worried since Clark has not been in touch since he left a day earlier to investigate some unusual meteor showers. The elder Kent assures her that their foster son should be home soon.

The next day, while flying back to Earth, Superboy runs into a huge meteor shower and is battered by the fragments. He starts tumbling through the air, lands on the ground and bounces. He struggles unsteadily to his feet, his expression dazed. (See illustration at left.) Superboy mutters to himself that the fragments must have been Red Kryptonite, which affects him in unpredictable ways. His mind gets fuzzy, so he quickly changes to his secret identity of Clark Kent.

Meanwhile, Pete Broder and Sammy Deslo, two teenagers who appear to be juvenile delinquents, are speeding down a country road in a stolen convertible. Pete, who is at the wheel, continues to push the speedometer past eighty miles per hour. Sammy warns him to slow down, but Pete refuses and drives even faster. Clark emerges from behind a boulder, and with a blank face, staggers out onto the road. Sammy pulls the key out o the ignition as the car roars by Clark, narrowly missing him. As the convertible slows to a stop, the boys agree to go back and pick up Clark. They back the car to where he is standing and ask him his name. Young Kent replies that he can't remember his name <u>or</u> where he is going, and gets in the car.

Soon the car is up to eighty miles an hour, when the boys encounter a motorcycle policeman, who pulls them over for speeding. Later the three boys are taken to the office of the State Correctional Honor Farm #2. Charlie Jones, the farm's manager, explains to the boys that they will be housed in the minimum security facility and that escape is futile since they are a hundred miles out in the country. Sammy and Peter both claim the car theft to be Clark's idea. When asked about this by Mr. Jones, Clark replies that he can't remember anything. After the other two boys leave, Jones tells Kent that he is registered as John Doe until he remembers his name.

Meanwhile, at the Kent house, Jonathan and Martha attempt to conceal their concern over Clark's absence, but in fact are both sick with worry. Kent reassures his wife that even if their son <u>were</u> in trouble, "he wouldn't forget them."

Back at the camp, Sammy and Pete declare themselves bosses of their dormitory. When they begin to bully a smaller teenager, Clark steps in and warns them to stop. Pete slugs Kent and only succeeds in hurting his wrist. As Sammy comments that Clark must be wearing steel muscles, the reference to unusual strength, causes young Kent's memory to return. He doesn't let on and asks the "bosses" permission to go outside. They agree and as soon as Clark is out of sight, he changes to Superboy and flies to the Kent home. He tells his relieved foster parents that he is serving a sentence on a State Honor Farm as a juvenile delinquent.

Back at the camp, Mr. Jones conducts the nightly bed check and finds "Joe Doe" missing. At the Kents, Superboy explains that he must return to camp so that Mr. Jones wouldn't have a black mark against him from an escape. He will stay until he can honorably leave.

Superboy returns to the farm and changes back to Clark. Kent is told to report to Jones' office, and there is informed that he is restricted to the dormitory for a month and that if he behaves, privileges will be restored.

Sammy and Pete have been cooperating with Jones to gain his confidence, and after being allowed to drive his car, have had a duplicate key made. Pete plans to short circuit the camp's electrical system that evening and in the confusion, steal Jones' car and escape. Clark overhears their plans but his efforts to stop them are temporarily foiled when Jones wants him to help with some bookkeeping.

That night, while the boys are sleeping, Pete orders Sammy to pull the switch at the fuse box. Sammy does this, and is immediately engulfed in sparks and knocked to the floor, unconscious. The farm's manager and Clark watch the lights go out. When Jones lights a match, he is astounded to see Superboy standing in front of him.

Back at the dorm, Sammy is still unconscious, with a live wire lying on top of him. Pete tells the panicked boys to back away, and grasps the wire in an effort to save his friend. He too, is knocked unconscious. Superboy arrives, removes the wires, and restores the fuse box to its original condition.

When Pete regains consciousness, he is told by Superboy that he is reformed since he risked his life to save his friend. Sammy and Pete agree to straighten up and fly right from now on. Pete admits to the farm manager that he lied about Clark's involvement with the stolen car. Jones replies that he is so sure that John Doe will "fly right," that he is being immediately released, and won't be seen again. Superboy wishes the boys luck and flies back to the Kent home.

SUPERBOY & SUPERPUP - THE LOST VIDEOS

SUPERBOY VS. SUPERBOY - {INT. THEATRE - BACK TO SUPERBOY - (FX)} - *He walks over to the piano.*
SUPERBOY: "I don't think we'll need this." *(He leans under the piano, lifts it easily and carries it out into the wings)* -
(Scene 40 - page 18)

THE SERIES THAT MIGHT HAVE BEEN

"SUPERBOY VS. SUPERBOY"
SUPERBOY #13

Written by
Vernon E. Clark and Whitney Ellsworth

The story begins in the apartment of Big Jake, a well dressed Syndicate man. Lefty Driscoll, another crook, and Ex-Doctor Damon, an older scientist, arrive at the apartment. Lefty tells Jake that Doc Damon is an energy expert who was paroled two weeks earlier from prison after serving a sentence for blasting open some safes. The word has been put out that the Syndicate is offering five hundred thousand dollars to anyone who can get rid of Superboy. Doc Damon says that he has a plan to store up Superboy's energy and use it to destroy him.

The next day at the Kent store, Lana Lang shows Clark a newspaper ad that requests a meeting with Superboy in Metropolis on the following Saturday. It is signed by James "Lefty" Driscoll.

That Saturday, Superboy shows up for the meeting and is asked by Lefty to put on a series of three exhibitions at a theater. Lefty hopes to accomplish three things: one, to make money, two, to enable Doc Damon to study Superboy in action, and three, to donate one thousand dollars per performance to Superboy's favorite charity. Superboy agrees and returns to Smallville, where he changes to Clark.

Later, at the Bijou Theatre, which will be used for the exhibitions, Doc Damon shows Lefty his energy sapping machine. It consists of a bank of batteries and a cable which runs from the master battery to the backstage area of the theater. The machine has intake and output switches which enable it to receive or discharge power.

That evening, the theater is packed as Superboy makes his first appearance. As Lefty introduces him, Superboy walks to a piano, lifts it with ease, and carries it out into the wings. (See illustration at left.) Backstage, the Doc watches his dial register reception of power. Superboy then welds two steel beams together with his bare hands to form a cross. The dial's needles register an even higher amount of energy. For his third stunt, Superboy runs through a brick wall that has been erected on the stage.

After the show, Lefty gives Superboy a thousand dollars for charity, reminding him the next day's performance is a matinee. After the Boy Of Steel leaves, Big Jake asks for a demonstration. The Doc disconnects the heavy cable from its antennae, aims it at the partial brick wall, and destroys what is left with a burst of energy. Lefty suggests using the device on Superboy as he flies in for the next day's matinee.

The following morning, as Superboy flies over Metropolis, the Doc aims the device's cable at the Boy Of Steel and fires. The ray's impact causes Superboy to fall to Earth, where he lies unconscious.

Believing the teen hero to be dead, the three crooks head toward the theater. Superboy soon recovers, and after arriving outside the theater, uses his X-ray vision and discovers the energy sapping machine. Lefty announces Superboy's absence to the crowd, when suddenly, the Boy Of Steel makes his entrance. The Doc whispers to Lefty that his machine hasn't stored enough power to defeat Superboy, but that after the next two exhibitions, it will.

Superboy runs through some more stunts and after the show, collects another one thousand dollars for charity. After he leaves, the Doc announces to his fellow crooks that after the next day's show he will be able to destroy Superboy for good.

The next day, Superboy returns for the final performance, and while performing the stunts, uses his X-ray vision to cause the machine's dial to register energy. Backstage, the Doc assures Lefty and Jake that the machine is now stronger than Superboy. After the show, Superboy is paid and returns to Smallville.

The following day, the Doc tells Lefty and Jake that they are going to use the energy machine to pull a bank robbery by melting a hole in the safe. When questioned about a possible confrontation with the police, Doc answers that any machine capable of destroying Superboy will be more than able to handle any cops.

Lefty calls Chief Parker in Smallville the next evening, and announces that the Central Bank in Metropolis will be robbed in twenty minutes and that Superboy should be told. Parker hangs up and calls Superboy on his special radio. Superboy tells Parker to call the Police Chief of Metropolis and tell him to keep his men away from the bank. There might be danger.

Meanwhile, at the bank, Doc aims his device at the safe's wall, which instantly melts. When the Boy Of Steel does arrive, the Doc aims his weapon. But before he can fire, Superboy uses his X-ray vision to melt the cable and destroy the energy machine.

Later, after the police have arrived and handcuffed the crooks, Superboy explains how he defeated their plan. He tells the Doc that the dials gave him the wrong information, and that he caused the dials to move while not expending energy on stage. He had substituted lightweight items for the third show so that the machine only had enough power to blast the bank's safe and couldn't harm the Boy Of Steel.

SUMMARY

The Adventures Of Superpup and *The Adventures Of Superboy* television pilots exist as unique examples of the vision of Whitney Ellsworth. This D.C. Comics pioneer, who made *The Adventures Of Superman* such a longstanding success and presented George Reeves as a hero to the baby boomer generations of the 1950's and 1960's, has accomplished much to be remembered for. His TV series is still being broadcast, with it being the second oldest in syndication after *I Love Lucy*, and a genuine classic of early television. Whit's early involvement with D.C. Comics helped establish them as a leader in their field, a position which continues to this day.

In conducting research for this book, I have encountered many kind and interesting people. They have all remembered Whitney Ellsworth with much fondness, and have expressed an interest in seeing the successful outcome of this project, since they all enjoyed seeing the pilots again. A well respected man who created such diversified contributions to popular culture and entertainment, certainly deserves to be remembered by the many children who benefitted from his artistic efforts. The two pilots, which have not been seen by many, due to unfortunate circumstances, are nonetheless interesting adaptations of the legend of the "Superman" character. Although not premiere examples of "Superman's" celluloid history, both "Superpup" and "Superboy" are entertaining and respectable efforts. "Superpup," which still appeals to those young children of the 1990's that have seen it, and "Superboy," with its superior production values and timely theme of parental pride and acceptance, are as worthy of viewing today as they were when first produced.

The "Superman" TV series, and the many superheroes that came from D.C. Comics, have always meant a great deal to me. From my youth to the present day, I have always known, that D.C. Comics and the "Superman" character, would provide me with much in the way of escapist entertainment.

This book, my first, is my opportunity to expose readers to these two lost television pilots (which still exist) and to say "thank you" for all those wonderful hours of happiness that have been given to me by the celluloid "Superman," the wonderful world of D.C. Comics, and particularly, Whit Ellsworth.

Chuck Harter
Hollywood, California
1993

ABOUT CHUCK HARTER

by Gwen Meades

Chuck took his first breath of salt-air in Tampa, Florida, where he was born on   . His Dad and Mom were <u>both</u> in the Air Force at the time. Service life being what it is, they eventually moved on -- to England! They lived there four years, and Chuck attended their schools. Over there, you don't just show up for class; you DO get an education. It's probably at least partially what he can contribute his "thinkability" to. The family finally got "orders" back to the States, and in time, ended up in Alexandria, Virginia. (His folks are still there.)

During the growing-up years, along with all the other usual childhood interests, Chuck listened to music, went to silent movies, and watched TV. And he read -- a <u>lot</u>. As reading and music and TV filled more and more of his time, he accumulated vast collections of books and tapes, and got to "know" the people in them; nearly as well as they knew themselves. He'd grown up with them. Chuck also spent much of his time in comic books, where he first got to know the super-heroes. Between the comics and the TV show, he became a life-long fan of "Superman." Not just any Superman -- George Reeves. He was for Chuck, as he was for many, many boys and girls, a true hero in every sense of the word. Always there, always fair, and <u>always</u> won out over bad.

photo by Michael J. Hayde

Chuck finished school, and even put in some college time. Over the years, he's performed live lead vocals and guitar with his own band, and recorded a number of songs; he even dabbled in songwriting. He then spent quite a few years doing sound engineering, and saw some really great bands that the populus missed because for one reason or another or several, they never made it big. Occasonally, though, fate went the other way, and he would be the sound man for bands nobody knew anything about at the time, who went on to become extremely famous and successful. His avid involvement with music fed him for a long time, and while most of that work was with rock music, his favorite music still remains the old jazz greats, the big bands, and early rock. He knows all about all of those folks, too. But it's never been to impress anybody, they simply were his companions along the way. Beyond and besides the music, Chuck's even managed considerable graphics, lay-up, and stat-camera work, creating expert newspapers, flyers, booklets, and the like. He's written several articles for various publications, drawing from his own great resources and personal knowledge of many, many performers -- not just their performing sides, but their intimate sides as well; what made them tick, and what affected their lives and careers, and led them in the various directions they ultimately went.

This accumulation of knowledge and reference brought about for Chuck, one of his greatest sources of pride. He was called in as a "Rock Archivist," to do a synopsis segment of insight into the developmental factors influencing the life and career of Elvis Presley, by the highly popular TV show, *Hard Copy*. Albeit brief, he got his first claim to fame on a nationally broadcast television show. It was a thrill.

All in all, life's been an amazing encounter of personalities and adventures for Chuck (some of which have made him truly appeciate his <u>real</u> friends). It's also made <u>him</u> a fascinating, highly literate person, with a wildy funny personality. Over the years, which for all of us become increasingly filled with "being a responsible adult," a lot of things fell by the wayside, but Chuck never stopped reading or listening to music. He's affectionately called "a walking museum" by some.

Some folks already know Chuck has long-been gathering research and photos for a book he's doing on George Reeves, as Superman <u>and</u> as George Reeves. That quest helped him get to know Whitney Ellsworth better, not only as the producer of the "Superman" show, but also as a very special man in his own right. And along this vein, he quite by chance came upon the knowledge of two pilots Whit had produced in keeping with our long-time friend, Superman. Amused at first, he uncovered more and more information and clues about them; and Whit. Eventually, it led him to extreme interest in the ever-continuing "legend," and in Whit Ellsworth. Finally, Chuck decided to do his first book by introducing all of you to the man who produced *The Adventures of Superman* and these "unknown" pilots, <u>and</u> the pilots themselves, along with several wonderful people who were part of it all. There's a lot of fun here, and some really special feelings and memories from the folks who were there. So enjoy the fact and fun and fantasy,

www.ingramcontent.com/pod-product-compliance
Lightning Source LLC
Chambersburg PA
CBHW081255170426
43198CB00017B/2793